Blockchain and Banking

Pierluigi Martino

Blockchain and Banking

How Technological Innovations Are Shaping the Banking Industry

palgrave
macmillan

Pierluigi Martino
Department of Economics and Management
University of Pisa
Pisa, Italy

ISBN 978-3-030-70969-3 ISBN 978-3-030-70970-9 (eBook)
https://doi.org/10.1007/978-3-030-70970-9

This Palgrave Pivot imprint is published by the registered company Springer Nature Switzerland AG
The registered company address is: Gewerbestrasse 11, 6330 Cham, Switzerland

Contents

1 Introduction: The Rise of Fintech 1
References 6

2 Blockchain Technology: Key Features and Main Applications 9
2.1 Introduction 9
2.2 The Fundamentals of Blockchain Technology 10
2.3 Blockchain Types and Classifications 17
2.4 Blockchain Applications 20
References 27

3 Blockchain Technology and the Banking Industry 33
3.1 Introduction 33
3.2 Blockchain as a Potential Risk for Banks 34
3.3 Blockchain and Banking Efficiency 38
3.4 Blockchain as a Source for New Products and Services 46
3.5 Blockchain and Financial Inclusion 47
3.6 Conclusions 48
References 49

4 Blockchain and Banking Business Models 53
4.1 Introduction 53
4.2 Technological Development and Business Model Innovation 54

4.3 *Blockchain and Innovation in the Banking Business Models* 55
4.4 *Banks' Approach to Blockchain's Challenges* 64
4.5 *Conclusions* 66
References 67

5 Regulation of Blockchain Technology: An Overview 71
5.1 *Introduction* 71
5.2 *Regulatory Issues and Cryptocurrencies* 72
5.3 *Regulation of Cryptocurrencies* 73
5.4 *Regulatory Issues and Blockchain's Distributed Ledger Technology* 84
5.5 *Regulators' Approach to the Adoption of Blockchain Technology* 84
5.6 *Conclusions* 92
References 94

6 Final Remarks 99
References 103

Index 105

List of Figures

Fig. 2.1	Example of a blockchain	12
Fig. 4.1	The business model canvas (Osterwalder and Pigneur 2010)	56
Fig. 4.2	Status of adoption of blockchain's distributed ledger technology by EU banks (*Source* Own processing of data from the EBA's [2019] risk assessment report of the European banking system)	65

CHAPTER 1

Introduction: The Rise of Fintech

Abstract Advances in telecommunications and information technology have had a significant impact on the banking industry over the past few years. The rise of the financial technology (fintech) sector has also played an important role, with new technologies like blockchain having the potential to change the whole banking industry in faster and more disruptive ways than ever before. This chapter outlines the context of this study, presents the book's structure and objective and highlights the main themes of all the other chapters.

Keywords Technological innovations · Fintech · Blockchain technology · Banking

The banking industry has undergone considerable changes over the past few decades, especially because of the boom in technology that has resulted from advances in telecommunications and information technology (IT). These advances have transformed banking products, services and processes (Berger 2003; Frame and White 2014; Frame et al. 2018). Faster computing and the widespread adoption of the Internet have produced a more efficient payment system with new payment tools and banking services (e.g. automated teller machines (ATMs), credit cards, electronic payments, Internet banking, etc.), while advances in IT (both

P. Martino, *Blockchain and Banking*,
https://doi.org/10.1007/978-3-030-70970-9_1

hardware and software) have led to more efficient and sophisticated ways for banks to leverage vast quantities of consumer and company data.

Nevertheless, as (ECB 2019) notes, we are entering a new digital age with technologies that have the potential to change the whole banking industry in faster and more disruptive ways than ever before. In particular, recent technological developments have brought about financial technology (fintech) sector, which covers digital innovations and technology-enabled business model innovations in the financial arena (Philippon 2016; He et al. 2017; Frame et al. 2018).

According to the Financial Stability Board's (FSB) (2017) working definition of fintech, it is a "technologically enabled financial innovation that could result in new business models, applications, processes or products with an associated material effect on financial markets and institutions and the provision of financial services". Examples of such innovations include distributed ledger technologies (DLTs), digital currencies, new digital advisory and trading systems, artificial intelligence and machine learning, peer-to-peer lending, equity crowdfunding and so on. According to Philippon (2016, p. 2), "such innovations can disrupt existing industry structures and blur industry boundaries, facilitate strategic disintermediation, revolutionise how existing firms create and deliver products and services, provide new gateways for entrepreneurship, democratize access to financial services, but also create significant privacy, regulatory and law enforcement challenges". The European Banking Authority (EBA) (2017) also underscores the potential for these new technological innovations and points out that they may create many benefits for consumers and organisations, including access to credit, improved comparability of products, access to a wider product range, availability of up-to-date information, tailored product offerings, reduced costs and consumer convenience. Thus, these innovations may contribute to a decline in costs, a reduction in information asymmetry and an increase in efficiency and competition and provide broader access to financial services by developing new ways to obtain funds. At the same time, however, these technologies can also pose new risks to the financial system, which policymakers, regulators and supervisors should consider to ensure the financial stability, safety and soundness of financial institutions, as well as consumer and investor protection.

Given the potential of fintech technologies and products, the industry has evolved significantly over the past few years and experienced a massive year of investment in 2018, with total global investment (across venture capital (VC), private equity (PE) and mergers and acquisitions (M&A)), more than doubling from $54.4 billion in 2017 to $141.0 billion in 2018 (KPMG 2020). This rise was driven mainly by the United States, Europe and Asia, as reported in KPMG's report (2020) on global investment trends in the fintech sector. The positive trend also continued in 2019, with global investment hitting $135.7 billion, a slight drop from the 2018 results, but still more than double any year before 2018, thereby highlighting the strength of the global fintech market.

An innovation that is central to the current fintech space is blockchain technology (Guo and Liang 2016; Philippon 2016; Iansiti and Lakhani 2017; Frame et al. 2018), the distributed ledger technology behind Bitcoin (and other cryptocurrencies). It represents a key investment area of fintech (KPMG 2020).

Blockchain has widely been acknowledged as a disruptive technology and a key source of future financial market innovation (Lewis et al. 2017) that could revolutionise our society and the new world economy (McKinsey 2016; Peters and Panayi 2016; Ross 2017). Born as the technology underlying Bitcoin (Nakamoto 2008) to record cryptocurrencies transactions, blockchain has become a technology that can facilitate the process of recording any transaction type and track the movement of any asset, thus finding applications in multiple areas (Ulieru 2016; Iansiti and Lakhani 2017; Yermack 2017; Tapscott and Tapscott 2017).

Although the initial scepticism about blockchain's original idea, i.e. blockchain used to launch cryptocurrencies, several financial institutions (including banks, insurers, etc.) around the world have focused on the DLT behind blockchain (i.e. blockchain without cryptocurrencies) over the past few years to examine how it may affect most of their business. Particularly for the banking industry, the reason for the growing interest in blockchain technology is its potential to create new opportunities for banks and because it poses new threats to their business (Buitenhek 2016; McDonald et al. 2016; Peters and Panayi 2016; Holotiuk et al. 2017; Lindman et al. 2017; Martino 2019). Many scholars and practitioners (Buitenhek 2016; Guo and Liang 2016; Peters and Panayi 2016) suggest that some of the problems linked to activities in financial services (e.g. the rising cost of operations, efficiency bottlenecks, transaction lags, fraud and operational risks) can be solved by applying blockchain's DLT. In particular, by enabling smart contracts, maintaining immutable logs of transactions and facilitating the real-time execution of transactions, blockchain can be used to change how banks provide financial services and, consequently, offer potential advantages (in terms of cost, speed and data integrity) over traditional methods of proving ownership. In turn, this may enhance traditional financial institutions' competitive edge (McKinsey 2016; KPMG 2017; Yermack 2017). Several of the world's biggest banks are looking for opportunities in this area (i.e. blockchain's DLT) by investing in and researching innovative blockchain applications. However, other studies (McDonald et al. 2016; Holotiuk et al. 2017) regard blockchain—particularly blockchain used to launch cryptocurrencies—as a new competitor that can threaten banks' business. According to these studies, blockchain technology and cryptocurrencies may allow consumers and suppliers to connect directly and form online networks, thus removing the need for "middlemen" like a bank (Holotiuk et al. 2017) and potentially undermining banks' traditional role in verifying and enabling transactions such as payments. Moreover, blockchain may provide new gateways for entrepreneurship by making it possible for (especially fintech) start-ups to provide banking services at lower costs (Philippon 2016; Tapscott and Tapscott 2017). This means that blockchain can increase competition in the industry and potentially undermine banks' profitability (Yeoh 2017).

Thus, existing literature suggests that blockchain may present new challenges and not only create opportunities for but also pose threats to banks. This is pushing banks to rethink their operations, business models and strategies. However, relevant literature is in still its infancy, and we have no clear understanding of blockchain technology's potential implications for banks (Zhao et al. 2016). This book expands the literature on blockchain technology in banking by providing new insights into the developments, trends and challenges of blockchain in the banking industry. Building on the results of a previous study I conducted (Martino 2019), this book aims to shed more light on the implications of blockchain technology for banks, exploring the potential impact on traditional banking business models. To this end, the book is structured as follows.

Chapter 2 provides an overview of blockchain technology and highlights its key features, benefits and disadvantages. It also examines the different types of blockchain (i.e. private vs public blockchains), as well as their evolution (i.e. blockchain 1.0 vs blockchain 2.0 onwards). Finally, the chapter discusses the topic of cryptocurrencies and smart contracts, which are the two main applications of blockchain technology.

Chapter 3 explores the potential implications of blockchain technology for the banking industry. This chapter builds on the results of a previous study I conducted,[1] which used qualitative-based interviews with three professional bankers from different European banks that are dealing with the challenges of blockchain, and discusses the advantages and risks that blockchain technology can hold for banks. It also identifies the main banking areas that can be affected by adopting this technology.

Chapter 4 explores the potential impact of blockchain's DLT on traditional banking business models. Building on the Business Model Canvas framework developed by Osterwalder and Pigneur (**2010**), this chapter discusses how blockchain technology can affect all the elements of a bank's business model, namely how banks generate profits, which customers they serve, which distribution channels they use and so on. Moreover, the chapter provides an overview of the current status of banks' adoption of the technology and highlights their approach to handling the challenges of blockchain.

Finally, Chapter 5 addresses regulatory issues for blockchain technology, given the crucial role of regulation in the development of this technology. In particular, the chapter outlines regulatory responses to blockchain around the world, with a specific focus on how US and EU authorities are tackling the key risks (e.g. privacy issues, financial crime, hacking, etc.) associated with this new technology. The chapter makes a distinction between the regulatory issues that derive from banks applying the DLT of blockchain when providing their services and the use of blockchain to launch cryptocurrencies, as they have very different implications.

The final section (Final remarks) provides a concluding discussion of the study by highlighting the main findings.

[1] Martino, P. (2019). Blockchain technology: Challenges and opportunities for banks. *International Journal of Financial Innovation in Banking*, *2*(4), 314–333. https://dx.doi.org/10.1504/IJFIB.2019.104535. Inderscience Enterprises Ltd. retains the copyright of the original article.

References

Berger, A. N. (2003). The economic effects of technological progress: Evidence from the banking industry. *Journal of Money, Credit and Banking, 35*(2), 141–176.

Buitenhek, M. (2016). Understanding and applying blockchain technology in banking: Evolution or revolution? *Journal of Digital Banking, 1*(2), 111–119.

EBA. (2017). *Discussion paper on the EBA's approach to financial technology* (FinTech). Available at: https://eba.europa.eu/sites/default/documents/files/documents/10180/1919160/7a1b9cda-10ad-4315-91ce-d798230ebd84/EBA%20Discussion%20Paper%20on%20Fintech%20%28EBA-DP-2017-02%29.pdf.

ECB. (2019). *Lending and payment systems in upheaval: The fintech challenge*. Speech by Yves Mersch, Member of the Executive Board of the ECB, at the 3rd annual Conference on Fintech and Digital Innovation, 26 February 2019, Brussels. Available at: https://www.ecb.europa.eu/press/key/date/2019/html/ecb.sp190226~d98d307ad4.en.html.

Frame, W. S., & White, L. J. (2014). Technological change, financial innovation, and diffusion in banking. In A. N. Berger, P. Molyneux & J. O. S. Wilson (Eds.), *The oxford handbook of banking, second edition* (pp. 1–5). Oxford University press.

Frame, W. S., Wall, L. D., & White, L. J. (2018). *Technological change and financial innovation in banking: Some implications for fintech*. Federal Reserve Bank of Atlanta, Working paper series. Available at: https://www.frbatlanta.org/-/media/documents/research/publications/wp/2018/11-technological-change-and-financial-innovation-in-banking-some-implications-for-fintech-2018-10-02.pdf.

FSB. (2017). *Financial stability implications from FinTech*. Supervisory and regulatory issues that merit authorities' Attention, 27 June 2017. Available at: https://www.fsb.org/wp-content/uploads/R270617.pdf.

Guo, Y., & Liang, C. (2016). Blockchain application and outlook in the banking industry. *Financial Innovation, 2*(1), 24.

He, M. D., Leckow, M. R. B., Haksar, M. V., Griffoli, M. T. M., Jenkinson, N., Kashima, M. M., … & Tourpe, H. (2017). *Fintech and financial services: Initial considerations*. International Monetary Fund. Available at: https://www.imf.org/en/Publications/Staff-Discussion-Notes/Issues/2017/06/16/Fintech-and-Financial-Services-Initial-Considerations-44985.

Holotiuk, F., Pisani, F., & Moormann, J. (2017). *The impact of blockchain technology on business models in the payments industry*. In Proceedings of 13th International Conference on Wirtschaftsinformatik, St. Gallen, 12–15 February, pp. 912–926.

Iansiti, M., & Lakhani, K. R. (2017). The truth about blockchain. *Harvard Business Review, 95*(1), 119–127.

KPMG. (2017). *Blockchain in financial services: A threat or an opportunity*. Available at: https://home.kpmg.com/ng/en/home/insights/2017/06/blockchain-in-financial-services--athreat-or-an-opportunity.html.

KPMG. (2020). *Pulse of Fintech H2 2019*, February 2020. Available at: https://assets.kpmg/content/dam/kpmg/xx/pdf/2020/02/pulse-of-fintech-h2-2019.pdf.

Lewis, R., McPartland, J., & Ranjan, R. (2017). Blockchain and financial market innovation. *Economic Perspectives, 41*(7), 1–17, Federal Reserve Bank of Chicago.

Lindman, J., Tuunainen, V. K., & Rossi, M. (2017). *Opportunities and risks of blockchain technologies—A research agenda*. In Hawaii International Conference on System Sciences (HICSS). Available at: https://hdl.handle.net/10125/41338.

MacDonald, T. J., Allen, D. W., & Potts, J. (2016). Blockchains and the boundaries of self-organized economies: Predictions for the future of banking. *Banking beyond banks and money* (pp. 279–296). Cham: Springer.

Martino, P. (2019). Blockchain technology: Challenges and opportunities for banks. *International Journal of Financial Innovation in Banking, 2*(4), 314–333.

McKinsey & Company. (2016). *How blockchains could change the world*. Available at: https://www.mckinsey.com/industries/high-tech/our-insights/how-blockchains-could-changethe-world.

Nakamoto, S. (2008). *Bitcoin: A peer-to-peer electronic cash system*. Available at: https://bitcoin.org/bitcoin.pdf.

Osterwalder, A., & Pigneur, Y. (2010). *Business model generation: A handbook for visionaries, game changers, and challengers*. John Wiley & Sons.

Peters, G. W., & Panayi, E. (2016). Understanding modern banking ledgers through blockchain technologies: Future of transaction processing and smart contracts on the internet of money. *Banking beyond banks and money* (pp. 239–278). Cham: Springer.

Philippon, T. (2016). *The fintech opportunity* (No. w22476). National Bureau of Economic Research working paper series. Available at: https://www.nber.org/system/files/working_papers/w22476/w22476.pdf.

Ross, E. S. (2017). Nobody puts blockchain in a corner: The disruptive role of blockchain technology in the financial services industry and current regulatory issues. *Catholic University Journal of Law and Technology, 25*(2), 7.

Tapscott, A., & Tapscott, D. (2017). How blockchain is changing finance. *Harvard Business Review, 1*(9), 2–5.

Ulieru, M. (2016). Blockchain 2.0 and beyond: Adhocracies. In *Banking Beyond Banks and Money* (pp. 297–303). Cham: Springer.

Yeoh, P. (2017). Regulatory issues in blockchain technology. *Journal of Financial Regulation and Compliance, 25*(2), 196–208.

Yermack, D. (2017). Corporate governance and blockchains. *Review of Finance, 21*(1), 7–31.

Zhao, J. L., Fan, S., & Yan, J. (2016). Overview of business innovations and research opportunities in blockchain and introduction to the special issue. *Financial Innovation, 2*, 28. Available at: https://doi.org/https://doi.org/10.1186/s40854-016-0049-2.

CHAPTER 2

Blockchain Technology: Key Features and Main Applications

Abstract This chapter provides a general overview of the fundamentals of blockchain technology and how it works. The goal is to make it clear why this technology is considered disruptive. In particular, the chapter discusses the key features of blockchain technology and its various types and categories; it also highlights their different characteristics, advantages and risks. Moreover, it explores the two main applications of blockchain, namely cryptocurrencies and smart contracts.

Keywords Blockchain · Distributed ledger technology · Cryptocurrencies · Smart contracts

2.1 Introduction

Many scholars and financial players agree that blockchain is a disruptive technology and a key source of innovation in financial markets in the future and that it could revolutionise our society and the new world economy. Since its start as the technology underlying Bitcoin and its use in recording cryptocurrency transactions, blockchain has become a technology that can both facilitate the process of recording any transaction type and track the movement of any asset. Its application is widespread and in different areas.

P. Martino, *Blockchain and Banking*,
https://doi.org/10.1007/978-3-030-70970-9_2

This chapter provides a general overview of the fundamentals of blockchain technology and how it works. The goal is to make it clear why this technology is considered disruptive. In particular, the chapter discusses the key features of blockchain technology and its various types and categories; it also highlights their different characteristics, advantages and risks. Moreover, it explores the two main applications of blockchain, namely cryptocurrencies and smart contracts.

2.2 The Fundamentals of Blockchain Technology

Blockchain is a digital, decentralised and distributed ledger that is constantly updated. This technology makes it possible to record transactions and track assets in a given network (Swan 2015; Crosby et al. 2016; Walport 2016). The word "blockchain" comes from the transactions being grouped into "blocks" (as a data package), which are linked to the blocks that precede them to form a chronological "chain" of blocks. This blockchain provides a trail of the underlying transaction and, thus, represents a complete ledger of the transaction history (Holotiuk et al. 2017; Nofer et al. 2017). However, unlike traditional ledgers, blockchain combines several computer technologies, including a digital ledger, distributed data storage, point-to-point transmission, consensus mechanisms and encryption algorithms (Guo and Liang 2016; Holotiuk et al. 2017; Lewis et al. 2017), which offer potential advantages in terms of cost, speed and data integrity. In particular, it is possible to identify some key features that underlie blockchain and make it a disruptive technology (Bohme et al. 2015; Iansiti and Lakhani 2017; Tapscott and Tapscott 2017; Zheng et al. 2017; Martino et al. 2019).

First, blockchain is a "distributed ledger" of a network's participants, and all the participants have permission to access it. "Distributed" means that every participant can share a ledger that is updated every time a transaction occurs and has simultaneous access to view the information[1] (Natarajan et al. 2017). Thus, transparency is assured in blockchain as the complete transaction history is stored by all the participants on a network and is visible to anyone with access to the system (Fanning and

[1] Basically, there is only one version of the ledger, and each network participant owns a full and up-to-date copy of the entire ledger. As a result, every addition to the ledger by a network participant is propagated to all nodes; upon validation, the new transaction is added to all the relevant ledgers to ensure data consistency across the network.

Centers 2016; Iansiti and Lakhani 2017). At the same time, it is also "decentralised" because no individual node can fully control the entire network (Iansiti and Lakhani 2017; Tapscott and Tapscott 2017). Hence, no central authority is required as control over the ledger is given to all the network participants. The decentralised storage in blockchain also ensures high robustness by eliminating a single point of failure, which is typical of centralised systems (Fanning and Centers 2016). Indeed, if there is a failure in any node, the other nodes will continue to operate, thereby maintaining the system's availability.

Second, blockchain uses "peer-to-peer technology", which allows users to connect without a central point of authority or control (Iansiti and Lakhani 2017; Tapscott and Tapscott 2017). This allows for decentralised transaction processing, meaning that everyone can directly send something to anyone else in a given network, thus removing the need for a central authority to verify trust and to transfer something of value.

Third, as mentioned above, in the blockchain, transactions are grouped in blocks that are linked to the blocks that precede them, and this chronological chain of blocks provides a trail of the underlying transactions. These blocks are "cryptographically" sealed in the chain using hash functions, a type of cryptography system that converts an input of letters and numbers into an encrypted output of a fixed length (i.e. the "hash"), which cannot be inverted to recover the original input (Narayanan et al. 2016; Yermack 2017). Specifically, as shown in Fig. 2.1, in addition to the information on the transaction, each block contains the *hash value*[2] (i.e. a numeric value of a fixed length that uniquely identifies data) of the preceding block (parent), a *timestamp* that records the temporal existence of a particular blockchain ledger item at a given instance in time and a *nonce*, which is a random number used to verify the hash (Nomura Research Institute [NRI] 2016; Nofer et al. 2017; Zheng et al. 2018).

As a result, blocks are "chained" together: the header of each block includes a hash function that reflects the contents of the previous block, which itself includes a hash function derived from its predecessor and so on—all the way back to the first block in the chain (Yermack 2017). Furthermore, a block's transactions are hashed through the *Merkle root*, that is, the hash of all the hashes of all the transactions that are part of a block in a blockchain network (Martino et al. 2019). This means that the

[2] The cryptographic hash function produces the hash value, which ensures the authenticity of each transaction before it is added to the block.

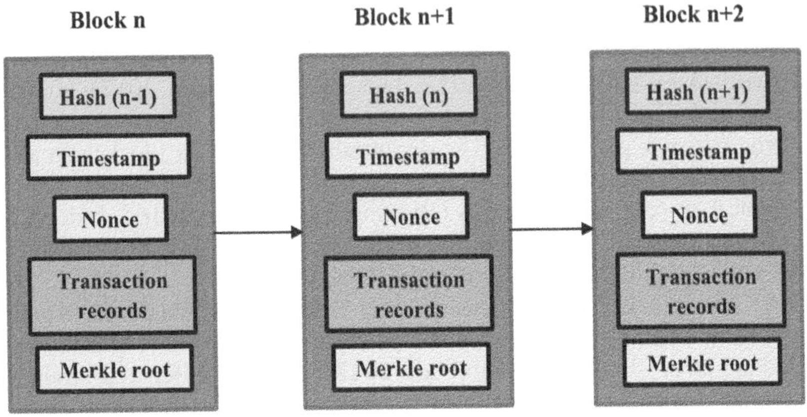

Fig. 2.1 Example of a blockchain

integrity and security of the information on the blockchain are ensured via cryptographic functions; this ensures the irreversibility of records and, consequently, high robustness and high trust since it is impossible to delete or edit these blocks (Iansiti and Lakhani 2017; Tapscott and Tapscott 2017; Adhami et al. 2018).

Blockchain also makes use of "asymmetric cryptography" mechanisms (i.e. public-key cryptography) to validate the authentication of transactions. This helps users to protect their digital property and enhance user security by using different keys for encryption and decryption: one for private use—i.e. a ***private key***—and one available to anyone—i.e. a ***public key*** (NRI 2016; Zheng et al. 2018). While a public key represents an individual's account address, which can be seen by anyone, a private key restricts access to account ownership to the private key/account holder.[3] The private—and public-key pairs allow people to encrypt the information that will be sent, thus enabling the receiver to determine whether the message originated with the right person and whether there has been any tampering (Peters and Panayi 2016). Thus, delivery and receipt of information can be done safely, since it is nearly impossible to derive

[3] A public key is similar to a bank account number, that is, public and available for the counterpart in a transaction (e.g. in the transfer of money). Conversely, a private key is similar to a bank account password: it is known and allows access only to the account holder.

a private key from its paired public key alone. Furthermore, when an account holder authorises a transaction, a "digital signature" is created through a mathematical algorithm. This signature combines users' private key with the data that they would like to transfer and is used to prove the authenticity of the data being sent. It is made by encrypting the hash value of the data to be sent with the sender's private key and is sent to the receiver together with these data. After receiving the data with the digital signature, the receiver uses the same hash function as the sender to generate the data's hash value and cross-checks the created hash value with the hash value obtained by decrypting the sender's digital signature with the sender's public key, thereby confirming the authenticity of the digital signature (NRI 2016; Drescher 2017).

Finally, another key characteristic of blockchain is that it is "consensus-based", that is, a transaction can be recorded only if all the participants in the network approve it (Lewis et al. 2017). Swanson (2015) defines the consensus mechanism as the process by which a majority (or, in some cases, all) of the network validators agree on the state of a ledger. According to him, "it is a set of rules and procedures that allows maintaining a coherent set of facts between multiple participating nodes". This means that a new block can be added to the chain when the majority of nodes in the network agree via a consensus mechanism on the validity of transactions in a block and on the validity of the block itself[4] (Nofer et al. 2017). Once validated, the new block is added to the blockchain, which essentially results in an update of the transaction ledger distributed across the network. Hence, in this system, every transaction is recorded in the ledger only after a verification process that ensures the transaction's validity, thus making blockchain a mechanism that ensures transparency and trust (Buitenhek 2016; Crosby et al. 2016).

There are several approaches to reach consensus in the blockchain, each of which has different advantages and disadvantages. The first and most popular blockchain consensus mechanism is Proof of Work (PoW), which is used in the Bitcoin network. In a PoW system, network participants have to solve a complex mathematical problem before they are allowed to add new "blocks" to the blockchain. They have to calculate

[4] Specifically, the consensus process ensures that transactions are stored in a block for a certain time (depending on the blockchain—for instance, 10 minutes in the Bitcoin blockchain) before being transferred to the ledger. After this period, the information in the blockchain can no longer be changed.

the hash value of the changing block header by using a random number (a nonce) until they achieve a value equal to or less than a specified target[5] (Zheng et al. 2018). When the relevant value is achieved, network participants should mutually confirm the correctness of the value; if the majority of participants agree on it, the new block is considered valid and is added to the existing chain. The miner who produces a valid PoW may receive cryptocurrency as a reward (e.g. in the form of a transaction fee), which serves as an economic incentive to maintain system integrity (Natarajan et al. 2017). It should be noted that, since the difficulty level of mining increases over time as more blocks are solved, the PoW mechanism requires a vast amount of computing resources, which entails high electricity costs and, consequently, high costs for the miner (Houben and Snyers 2018).

The second-best-known and most commonly used consensus mechanism is the Proof of Stake (PoS), which represents an energy-saving alternative to PoW where miners have to prove the ownership of the amount of currency (in the case of cryptocurrencies) to participate in the validation of transactions[6] (Houben and Snyers 2018; Zheng et al. 2018). While PoW depends on "computing power" to mine blocks, PoS depends on a node's "stake" in the system—typically, the amount of currency a user holds. This means a transaction validator will have to prove their "stake" (i.e. their share) of all coins in existence before they are allowed to validate a transaction. As a result, the greater the user's stake is, the more authority they have over validation, since they have greater seniority within the network, which earns them a more trusted position (Natarajan et al. 2017; Houben and Snyers 2018). An evolution of PoS is the Delegated Proof of Stake (DPoS), where the miners' ability to validate a block depends on their stake but, unlike with PoS, stakeholders (based on their stake) elect a group of delegated witnesses who generate and validate blocks (Li et al. 2017; Zheng et al. 2018).

[5] This process is commonly referred to as "mining", and the nodes that calculate the hashes are called "miners".

[6] This act of validating transactions is called "forging".

2.2.1 Blockchain Technology: Advantages and Disadvantages

Blockchain technology has been recognised as an alternative to the traditional financial ledgers based on classical double-entry bookkeeping (Yermack 2017). In particular, the distributed ledger technology behind the blockchain represents a break from the centralised data repositories that have historically used by companies to support transaction processing.

Traditionally, the databases for recording transactions have been centralised systems. Such systems are expensive, duplicate efforts, require long times and have many problems, especially regarding trust—i.e. they require third-party verification (MacDonald et al. 2016). The actors sharing a database have to trust a central authority, which controls a master copy, to keep the records accurate and maintain the technological infrastructure necessary to prevent data loss in case of equipment failure or cyberattacks. Accordingly, centralised systems are also vulnerable, since the central authority represents a single point of failure (Lewis et al. 2017); this means that if the central authority's technological infrastructure is compromised, the database is lost, which would affect the entire business network.

By combining several computer technologies, such as a digital ledger, distributed data storage, point-to-point transmission, consensus mechanisms and encryption algorithms, blockchain may solve the problems of traditional databases (i.e. centralised systems) by allowing fast, low-cost and secure transactions without the need for third parties (Buitenhek 2016; Yermack 2017). In particular, literature has identified the following advantages of blockchain technology (Iansiti and Lakhani 2017; Natarajan et al. 2017; Tapscott and Tapscott 2017; Zheng et al. 2018; Martino et al. 2019):

- *Decentralisation* and *disintermediation*. Blockchain enables decentralised transaction processing and record-keeping, thereby allowing anyone to directly transact and forge agreements without needing a central authority or an intermediary to verify trust and transfer something of value. This may lead to lower transaction costs.
- *Greater transparency*. Since the complete transaction history on the blockchain is stored by all participants on the network and it is visible to anyone with access to the system (all network participants have a full copy of the distributed ledger and, thus, complete access to

viewing the information), blockchain ensures greater transparency and, consequently, may reduce fraud.

- *Automation*. By automating parts of organisations' business processes, for instance by enabling the execution of a smart contract (see Sect. 2.4.2.), blockchain may significantly improve the efficiency of many organisation areas, such as compliance, by reducing the time and effort (and, therefore, costs) that organisations spend on those processes, as well as improving their quality, accuracy and speed.
- *Immutability*. Since information on the blockchain is secured by methods of cryptographic proof (Yermack 2017), meaning that once a transaction is entered in the database and the accounts are updated, the records cannot be altered because they are linked to every transaction record that preceded them, blockchain can provide an immutable and verifiable audit trail of transactions of any asset type.
- *Better cybersecurity resilience*. Thanks to its distributed nature, which removes the single point of attack or failure (Nofer et al. 2017), blockchain may provide a more resilient system than traditional centralised databases and offer better protection against different types of cyberattacks.

Nevertheless, the technology is still evolving, and many technological and regulatory issues have yet to be addressed. In particular, blockchain faces the following risks and challenges (Barber et al. 2012; Natarajan et al. 2017; Zheng et al. 2018; Martino et al. 2019)[7]:

- *Scalability*. Compared with traditional systems, blockchain (particularly public blockchains) faces issues related to scalability, in terms of both transaction volume and verification speed. For example, while public blockchain (on which Bitcoin operates) can only process between four and seven transactions per second because the block size is restricted to 1 megabyte, traditional banking systems today carry out thousands of operations per second.
- *Security issues*. Although it has largely been acknowledged that blockchain is secure, there are potential risks because of flaws in the technology (or, for example, the vulnerability of smart contracts),

[7] Many of these problems relate to public blockchains, and most of them are solved with private blockchains, as explained in the next paragraph.

which may lead to theft and cyberattacks, as several events over the past few years have shown[8] (see, for instance, the attack on the decentralised autonomous organisation known as The DAO, where hackers stole a third of the DAO's assets, valued at approximately $50 million) (Niranjanamurthy et al. 2018).

- *Privacy*. In public blockchains, all network participants can have access to a transaction's information, which generates privacy concerns. For instance, as De Filippi (2016) notes, the transparency inherent in blockchain "is such that anyone can retrieve the history of all transactions performed on a blockchain and rely on big data analytics in order to retrieve potentially sensitive information".
- *Environmental issues*. When using PoW as a consensus mechanism, blockchain creates potential environmental issues owing to the vast amounts of computing processing power needed for mining, as well as the frequent hardware update requirements that generate high electricity costs.

2.3 Blockchain Types and Classifications

Depending on the nature of the ledger, blockchain can be classified into three categories, namely ***public***, ***private*** and ***hybrid*** blockchains, each of which has its own characteristics in terms of consensus determination, read permission and degree of decentralisation (Peters and Panayi 2016; Natarajan et al. 2017; Zheng et al. 2018; Martino et al. 2019).

Public (also called ***permissionless***) blockchains are completely decentralised and have no single owner. Moreover, approval by a central entity is not required to join the network. Hence, any network participant may have access to information in and make transactions on the blockchain, as well as take part in the consensus process. Bitcoin and Ethereum are the best-known examples of a public blockchain. Conversely, in fully private (also called ***permissioned***) blockchains, a single entity, as owner or administrator of the ledger, sets the rules for the blockchain (Natarajan et al. 2017), has ownership, controls the whole blockchain (thus, it determines the final consensus) and designates who can participate in the network and in what capacity. Therefore, only permission holders (e.g.

[8] The "51% vulnerability" (or 51% attack) is one of the best-known risks in blockchain technology, where a participant may gain control of over 50% of a network's hashrate in order to act to benefit themselves at the expense of everyone else.

users within an organisation, or a group of organisations) can operate on the blockchain, since prior authorisation from a centralised authority is required to participate in the network (Peters and Panayi 2016). Examples of permissioned blockchain are Ripple and Corda (the latter was created by R3, a consortium of over 70 financial institutions). Generally, while *public* blockchains are those in which cryptocurrencies operate, private blockchains are used for specific usage cases, such as applications in the financial sector. It is also worth noting that private blockchains can overcome some of the drawbacks of blockchain discussed in the previous paragraph. In particular, by limiting the number of participants and the scope of consensus, which requires lower costs and computational power to work than public blockchains, private blockchains can achieve better scalability and processing speed and, consequently, ensure more efficiency (Martino 2019). Moreover, since a private blockchain is a closed system between predefined participants, it does not suffer from the regulatory issues (e.g. privacy concerns) faced by public blockchains.

Between the two extremes (public and private blockchains), a third classification that combines the two models is the hybrid (or *consortium*) blockchain, where the consensus process is controlled by a preselected set of nodes (Peters and Panayi 2016). Specifically, part of the network has the characteristic of being public (i.e. accessible to any participant), but only a privileged group is responsible for the consensus process. Thus, they are partially decentralised as the blockchain is only distributed among entitled participants.

A further classification of blockchain technology depends on its evolution and the development of its applications. The first application of blockchain was as a method of validating ownership of the virtual currency Bitcoin. However, while blockchain technology is often associated with digital or virtual currency schemes and payments, its scope is much wider: today, blockchain's distributed ledger technology can facilitate the recording of any transaction type and can track the movement of any asset, whether tangible, intangible or digital, and can be applied in multiple areas (Tapscott and Tapscott 2017). Depending on its evolution and the development of its applications, it is possible to identify different categories of blockchain technology: *Blockchain 1.0*, *Blockchain 2.0* and *Blockchain 3.0* (Swan 2015; Gatteschi et al. 2018; Martino et al. 2019).

Blockchain 1.0 is currency. It represents the first application of the technology, that is, the development of cryptocurrencies (e.g. Bitcoin) that relate to cash and digital payment systems. Specifically, it is the technology in which Bitcoin operates and that allows the recording of transactions in Bitcoin and other cryptocurrencies. Conversely, Blockchain 2.0 refers to the wide range of economic and financial applications beyond currency and simple payments (Efanov and Roschin 2018). According to Swan (2015), while Blockchain 1.0 is for the decentralisation of money and payments, Blockchain 2.0 is for the decentralisation of markets more generally and contemplates the transfer of many other kinds of assets beyond currency using blockchain. Applications in this fields include traditional banking instruments such as loans and mortgages, complex financial market instruments such as stocks, bonds, futures and derivatives, as well as legal instruments like titles, contracts and other assets and property that can be monetised.

Blockchain 2.0 is linked particularly to the development of smart contracts (Gatteschi et al. 2018), that is, programs written on the blockchain and executed automatically when certain conditions are met. They enable the operation of different types of applications, especially in the financial sector. The best-known example of Blockchain 2.0 is Ethereum, an open-source blockchain platform that allows developers to write smart contracts and decentralised applications (Dapps). These Dapps run on a network in a distributed manner with participant information securely protected and operation execution decentralised across network nodes[9] (Swan 2015).

Finally, Blockchain 3.0 refers to a vast array of applications that are beyond currency, finance and markets but have the potential to embrace various sectors such as government, health care, arts and education (Swan 2015; Crosby et al. 2016; Natarajan et al. 2017; Gatteschi et al. 2018). As the blockchain ecosystem matures, its use cases continue to increase far beyond financial applications. Over the past few years, several blockchain solutions have been developed in many different industries and for many reasons ranging from fraud protection and increased transparency to the reduction of transaction costs/fees and of counterparty risk.

[9] Within this context, it is also worth mentioning decentralised autonomous organisations (DAOs), which are organisations that are run through smart contracts by encoding the rules for making decisions and managing groups of people. These DAOs represent a more complex form of a decentralised application.

2.4 Blockchain Applications

As seen in the previous section, blockchain may be applied in a wide range of areas. This section focuses on the two main applications of blockchain technology, namely *cryptocurrencies* and *smart contracts*, and will highlight their characteristics and use cases.

2.4.1 Cryptocurrencies

Money has changed considerably throughout history—from bartering to using coins and paper money to, recently, paying digitally—thanks to technological advancements, some of which are now making cash-free transactions easier than ever before (OECD 2002; UBS 2018). With the advent of electronic payments, many actors all over the globe have moved away from cash transactions, making cashless transactions (i.e. digital forms of exchanging money, such as new mobile payments, credit/debit cards) ever more prevalent in the global economy, especially in emerging economies (Capgemini 2019). According to Capgemini's latest World Payments Report (2019), the number of non-cash transaction volumes around the world climbed 12% between 2016 and 2017 to reach 539 billion, with emerging markets leading the surge.

This shift may bring several benefits to the global economy in terms of efficiency gains, reducing tax evasion and so forth. At the same time, however, the emergence of new technologies gives rise to new issues related to fraud, money laundering, terrorism financing and cybercrime, which must be addressed. The rise of Bitcoin and other cryptocurrencies has added fuel to the discussion, given their potential to disrupt existing payment and monetary systems (Bohme et al. 2015).

Cryptocurrencies, which represent the pioneering application of blockchain technology, are digital financial assets (digital currencies) designed to work as a medium of exchange that uses cryptography, rather than a bank or other trusted third party (government or other central authority), to secure financial transactions, control the creation of additional units and verify the transfer of assets (Yermack 2013; European Payment Council 2019; Giudici et al. 2020).[10] They use decentralised control instead of centralised digital currency and central banking systems

[10] To date, there has been no generally accepted definition of the term cryptocurrency in the regulatory space, although policymakers are trying to define it (see Chapter 5).

(Bohme et al. 2015; Richter et al. 2015; Jacobs 2018). In particular, in contrast to traditional fiat currencies, which require a central trusted party (e.g. the central bank) to guarantee the value of national currencies and transactions, cryptocurrencies rely on blockchain technologies to create a distributed system of certification and integrity on the Internet for payment transactions, thereby eliminating the need for a central authority (Adhami et al. 2018).

Bitcoin is the first and best-known cryptocurrency. It arrived on the scene in 2008 when an individual or group of developers using the pseudonym Satoshi Nakamoto drafted a whitepaper to propose the creation of a peer-to-peer electronic cash system (i.e. Bitcoin) whose purpose would be to allow online payments to be sent directly from one party to another without going through a financial institution (Nakamoto 2008). The idea was to create an electronic payment system based on cryptographic proof instead of trust, which allows anyone to transact and transfer value directly to another party without the need for a trusted third party such as banks, thus solving the issue of needing a third party when making a payment.[11]

A host of digital currencies have subsequently been created, and dedicated (trading) platforms have been established over the years to exchange fiat money for cryptocurrencies and vice versa. At present, there are over 2,000 cryptocurrencies (also called altcoins)[12] with a total market capitalisation of more than €300 billion.[13] The most popular ones are Ethereum,[14] Ripple, Litecoin, Bitcoin Cash, Dash and Monero, to name

[11] As mentioned in the previous paragraphs, Bitcoin is a typical example of an open, permissionless blockchain based on a PoW consensus mechanism. To use Bitcoin (and any other cryptocurrency), users need a digital wallet—a software program that stores private and public keys and interacts with various blockchains—to send and receive digital currency and monitor their balance.

[12] Cryptocurrencies can be divided into categories, namely coins and tokens. According to Massey et al. (2017), coins are units of value that are native to a particular blockchain and whose objective is to exchange value. Other than that, they have limited functionality, whereas tokens can have functionality beyond an exchange of value, since they can represent any asset or functionality that the developer desires.

[13] According to data available on https://coinmarketcap.com (data accessed in October 2020).

[14] According to the Payment Methods Report (2019), Ether, which is used as a form of payment in the Ethereum platform, was the most-used cryptocurrency in daily transactions in the fourth quarter of 2018.

just a few. It is worth noting that some of these new cryptocurrencies solve many problems inherent in Bitcoin, thus enabling significant improvements and advancing the development of cryptocurrencies in general (Martino et al. 2019).

The market for cryptocurrencies has grown massively since 2008 in terms of the number of new currencies, as well as the consumer base and the transaction frequency (Dyhrberg 2016). As reported in the Payment Methods Report (2019) by the European Payments Council, the number of payments made by using cryptocurrencies is constantly on the rise, with several companies (Microsoft and Expedia, among others) accepting Bitcoin and other cryptocurrencies, and others allowing customers to make Bitcoin payments via crypto payment gateways such as BitPay. The potential of cryptocurrencies, which can explain their current economic value, is substantial and linked particularly to the fact that they may ease financial transactions by providing more flexibility and speed in international transfer than other currencies managed by banks (Dyhrberg 2016). As the main determinant of the value of cryptocurrencies, literature points to: the high speed and low cost of transactions because of the elimination of intermediaries, for example; greater accessibility to everyone connected to the Internet, which fosters financial inclusion for unbanked and underbanked populations (the former are people without a bank account; the latter are people with limited access to traditional banking services and products); and greater privacy, which guarantees anonymity and security when making payments (Richter et al. 2015; Jacobs 2018; Giudici et al. 2020).

However, there are several factors—including inefficiency in transactions (technical/sscalability problems) and high volatility (Ciaian et al. 2016)—that currently limit the potential for broad adoption in day-to-day payments (UBS 2018). Hence, cryptocurrencies have to compete with other systems in terms of costs, speed and scalability. For example, new transaction technologies (such as SEPA Instant Credit Transfer) and fund transfer systems (such as Transferwise) make it possible to reduce costs and time in money transfer (the Instant scheme allows pan-European credit transfers, with the funds made available in less than 10 seconds). The security and privacy of cryptocurrencies have also been a topic of discussion. With respect to security issues, cryptocurrencies may be subject to theft and hacker attacks (e.g. if someone stole the user's private key and could then tamper with the user's account). Regarding privacy issues, Bohme et al. (2015) note that Bitcoin transactions are not truly anonymous but pseudonymous, given that each transaction specifies account information (i.e. the user's public key), albeit without personal names, and the blockchain publishes transactions with that user identifier. According to them, a Bitcoin user's identity could be obtained by exploiting such information (see also De Filippi 2016).

Moreover, cryptocurrencies have to overcome several regulatory hurdles (Jacobs 2018). The anonymity (or pseudonymity) and lack of regulation associated with cryptocurrencies have raised serious concerns, particularly regarding the use of cryptocurrencies for fraud, hacking, money laundering, terrorism financing and tax evasion (Bohme et al. 2015; Richter et al. 2015; Houben and Snyers 2018), among others. Regulators around the world are worried about criminals increasingly using cryptocurrencies for illicit activities. The rules of cryptocurrency exchange may change in the future because of the authorities' intervention in response to the problems above (Martino et al. 2019).

2.4.1.1 The Initial Coin Offerings Mechanism

Linked to cryptocurrencies, another application of blockchain technology is the Initial Coin Offerings (ICOs) mechanism, which represents a vehicle for obtaining financing for new start-ups, especially for blockchain-based organisations (Frame et al. 2018; Martino et al. 2019). Specifically, the ICOs mechanism represents a new fundraising model based on blockchain technology and related cryptocurrencies. It works similarly to crowdfunding but sells instruments of a different nature (tokens) and uses blockchain technology for verification instead of a crowdfunding platform[15] (Arnold et al. 2019; Fisch 2019).

Many scholars and financial players consider ICOs a key innovation in the entrepreneurial finance context (Howell et al. 2018; Martino et al. 2019) and regard them as an alternative to traditional financing (e.g. venture capital, angel investors and crowdfunding) because they offer several advantages for new ventures, as well as investors. A large number

[15] In an ICO, an organisation issues coins or tokens and puts them up for sale in exchange for traditional currencies (e.g. the euro) or, more often, virtual currencies (e.g. Bitcoin or Ether). The features and purpose of the coins or tokens vary across ICOs. For instance, some coins or tokens may serve to access or purchase a service or product that the issuer develops using the proceeds of the ICO; others may provide voting rights or a share in the future revenues of the issuing venture. Some may have no tangible value, while other coins or tokens may be traded and/or exchanged for traditional or virtual currencies at specialised coin exchanges after issuance (see ESMA 2017).

of companies and individuals are using ICOs more and more as a way to raise capital or participate in investment opportunities[16] (SEC 2017). As literature (e.g. Tapscott and Tapscott 2017; Howell et al. 2018; Fisch 2019; Huang et al. 2019; Martino et al. 2019, 2020) highlights, thanks to the key characteristics of blockchain technology, ICOs may enable new ventures to collect a large number of financial contributions from a significant number of investors across the world in a faster, more flexible way and at a lower cost than other traditional funding mechanisms such as crowdfunding. Moreover, they provide advantages for potential investors by reducing entry barriers to participate financially in successful start-ups, meaning that anyone (including small investors) can invest any amount in a company. However, ICOs do have some potentially risky shortcomings. Flaws in the blockchain technology can be subject to cyberattacks, and the lack of regulation can make investors vulnerable to fraud or increase illicit activities (Martino et al. 2020).[17]

2.4.2 Smart Contracts

A further key application of blockchain technology is *smart contracts*, that is, "computerized transaction protocol that executes the terms of a contract" according to computer scientist and cryptographer Nick Szabo, who first introduced the concept in 1994. The idea that he proposed was to translate contractual clauses into code and embed them in hardware or software that can self-enforce them (i.e. satisfy common contractual conditions) to minimise both the need for trusted intermediaries between transacting parties and the occurrence of malicious or accidental exceptions (Szabo 1994, 1997). Thus, they fundamentally represent contracts written in computer code that execute automatically once certain conditions specified in the contract are met[18] (Lewis et al. 2017). There is

[16] A new variant of ICOs has recently emerged, namely initial exchange offerings (IEOs). They rely on cryptocurrency exchanges to ensure the trustworthiness of potential projects and connect high-quality projects to potential investors (see, for example, Chen and Bellavitis 2020).

[17] For an overview of the main risks of investing in ICOs, see Martino et al. (2019) and (2020).

[18] The contracting parties agree on the code in advance and ensure that it takes their interests into account.

currently no established definition for smart contracts, and their official legal status remains somewhat unclear (Lauslahti et al. 2017). For instance, Lauslahti et al. (2017, p. 11) define smart contracts as "digital programs, based on the blockchain consensus architecture, which will self-execute when the terms of the agreement are met, and due to their decentralised structure are also self-enforcing and tamper-proof". In the same vein, Cong and He (2019, p. 1761) define smart contracts as "digital contracts allowing terms contingent on decentralized consensus that are tamper-proof and typically self-enforcing through automated execution".

Although the idea of smart contracts was developed in the 1990s, it was only with the emergence of blockchain technology that they became more popular. This is because blockchain can facilitate the execution of smart contracts better than the technology available at the time of their invention, since blockchain's distributed ledger technology makes it possible to host and automatically execute contracts using cryptography without the involvement of third parties (e.g. notaries, lawyers, etc.)[19] (Fairfield 2014; Nofer et al. 2017; Gatteschi et al. 2018; Giudici and Adhami 2019). Specifically, blockchain allows code to be embedded in the distributed ledger, thus making the contract tamper-resistant, and once specific predefined conditions are met, the contract self-executes automatically without the need for third parties to enforce the agreements between the parties, since neither party can tamper with the code (Wang et al. 2019).

Through the implementation of smart contracts, many (e.g. Nowinski and Kozma 2017; Cong and He 2019) believe that blockchain may disrupt the entire transaction process and can be expected to potentially affect traditional business as well, since smart contracts may allow the automation of processes that currently require manual intervention: specifically, they can enable the automatic execution of commercial transactions and agreements in a cost-efficient, transparent and secure way, in real time and without the involvement of a third party. As studies (Yermack 2017; Cong and He 2019) suggest, the potential applications of smart contracts are broad, particularly for the financial services industry. For instance, Cong and He (2019) claim that smart contracts can increase contractibility and facilitate the exchange of money, property,

[19] As mentioned in sub-Sect. 2.3, Ethereum is a prominent example of blockchain that supports the implementation of smart contracts.

shares, service or anything of value in an algorithmically automated way. Other studies (e.g. Capgemini 2016; Lewis et al. 2017) suggest that smart contracts may allow the automation of processes that currently require manual interventions and rely on physical documents; these processes are characterised by delays, inefficiencies and increased exposure to errors and fraud. According to a report by Capgemini (2016), the adoption of smart contracts could reduce risks, lower administration and service costs and provide more efficient business processes across all major segments of the financial services industry. For instance, its estimates suggest that mortgage borrowers in the US and European markets could potentially save between \$480 and \$960 per loan, and banks would be able to reduce costs in the range of \$3 billion to \$11 billion annually by lowering processing costs in the mortgage origination process. Other relevant areas for financial institutions, where the use of smart contracts can reduce the manual effort required to support the execution of economic transactions and, thus, accelerate business processes, include global payments, syndicated credit, cross-border settlement and trade finance, as well as regulatory and compliance activities (Swanson 2015; Capgemini 2016; Cong and He 2019).

Despite their numerous potentials mentioned above, smart contracts also pose several challenges that need to be tackled before they can reach widespread adoption (Peters and Panayi 2016). In addition to technical vulnerabilities, the use of smart contracts raises many legal and regulatory issues (Yermack 2017; Natarajan et al. 2017). First, smart contracts are vulnerable and may be subject to cyberattacks since they cannot be modified (the most relevant case of a smart contract-based attack is The DAO) (Gatteschi et al. 2018). In the hypothesis that a smart contract contains a bug, once the contract is stored on the blockchain, it can no longer be modified given the immutable nature of the blockchain, which means that there is no direct way to fix the bug (Atzei et al. 2017). As Gatteschi et al. (2018) suggest, developers should create a new contract and transfer all data and pointers from the old to the new ones in order to remove code bugs. Second, the lack of standards and regulations raises a number of legal and regulatory issues, particularly with regard to liability, jurisdiction, amendments and the voidability of contracts, as well as consequent concerns about the degree to which smart contracts can legally substitute paper agreements (Natarajan et al. 2017; Giudici and Adhami 2019). For instance, the immutability of smart contracts (i.e. they cannot be changed after they are deployed) may generate problems if external conditions change, such as changes to the law, applicable regulations and so forth, which would require a change in the smart contract, or if some event has a legal impact on the rights and obligations of the parties to the smart contract. Other problems may result from situations in which a court does not consider the outcome of a smart contract legal under existing law (Gatteschi et al. 2018). Hence, numerous technical and legal issues must be addressed to make smart contracts interoperate with the existing legal system (Lauslahti et al. 2017).

References

Adhami, S., Giudici, G., & Martinazzi, S. (2018). Why do businesses go crypto? An empirical analysis of initial coin offerings. *Journal of Economics and Business, 100,* 64–75.

Arnold, L., Brennecke, M., Camus, P., Fridgen, G., Guggenberger, T., Radszuwill, S., et al. (2019). Blockchain and initial coin offerings: Blockchain's implications for crowdfunding. *Business transformation through blockchain* (pp. 233–272). Cham: Palgrave Macmillan.

Atzei, N., Bartoletti, M., & Cimoli, T. (2017). *A survey of attacks on ethereum smart contracts* (sok). *Principles of security and trust* (pp. 164–186). Berlin, Heidelberg: Springer.

Barber, S., Boyen, X., Shi, E., & Uzun, E. (2012). *Bitter to better—How to make bitcoin a better currency*. International Conference on Financial Cryptography and Data Security. Springer, Heidelberg, 399–414.

Böhme, R., Christin, N., Edelman, B., & Moore, T. (2015). Bitcoin: Economics, technology, and governance. *Journal of Economic Perspectives, 29*(2), 213–238.

Buitenhek, M. (2016). Understanding and applying blockchain technology in banking: Evolution or revolution? *Journal of Digital Banking, 1*(2), 111–119.

Capgemini Consulting. (2016). *Smart contracts in financial services: Getting from hype to reality*, Technical Report. Available at: https://www.capgemini.com/consulting/wp-content/uploads/sites/30/2017/07/smart-contracts.pdf.

Capgemini. (2019). *World payments report 2019*. Available at: https://worldpaymentsreport.com/resources/world-payments-report-2019/.

Chen, Y., & Bellavitis, C. (2020). Blockchain disruption and decentralized finance: The rise of decentralized business models. *Journal of Business Venturing Insights, 13,* e00151.

Ciaian, P., Rajcaniova, M., & Kancs, D. A. (2016). The economics of BitCoin price formation. *Applied Economics, 48*(19), 1799–1815.

Cong, L. W., & He, Z. (2019). Blockchain disruption and smart contracts. *The Review of Financial Studies, 32*(5), 1754–1797.

Crosby, M., Pattanayak, P., Verma, S., & Kalyanaraman, V. (2016). BlockChain technology: Beyond Bitcoin. *Applied Innovation Review, 71*(2), 6–10.

De Filippi, P. (2016). The interplay between decentralization and privacy: The case of blockchain technologies. *Journal of Peer Production* (7).

Drescher, D. (2017). *Blockchain basics* (Vol. 276). Berkeley, CA: Apress.

Dyhrberg, A. H. (2016). Bitcoin, gold and the dollar–A GARCH volatility analysis. *Finance Research Letters, 16*, 85–92.

Efanov, D., & Roschin, P. (2018). The all-pervasiveness of the blockchain technology. *Procedia Computer Science, 123*, 116–121.

ESMA. (2017). *ESMA highlights ICO risks for investors and firms*. Available at: https://www.esma.europa.eu/press-news/esma-news/esma-highlights-ico-risks-investors-and-firms.

European Payment Council. (2019). *Payment methods report 2019. Innovations in the way we pay*. Available at: https://www.europeanpaymentscouncil.eu/sites/default/files/inline-files/Payment%20Methods%20Report%202019%20-%20Innovations%20in%20the%20Way%20We%20Pay.pdf.

Fairfield, J. A. (2014). Smart contracts, bitcoin bots, and consumer protection. *Wash. & Lee L. Rev. Online, 71*, 35.

Fanning, K., & Centers, D. P. (2016). Blockchain and its coming impact on financial services. *Journal of Corporate Accounting and Finance, 27*(5), 53–57.

Fisch, C. (2019). Initial coin offerings (ICOs) to finance new ventures. *Journal of Business Venturing, 34*(1), 1–22.

Frame, W. S., Wall, L. D., & White, L. J. (2018). *Technological change and financial innovation in banking: Some implications for fintech*, Working Paper No. 2018–11, FRB Atlanta. Available at: https://www.frbatlanta.org/-/media/documents/research/publications/wp/2018/11-technological-change-and-financial-innovation-in-banking-some-implications-for-fintech-2018-10-02.pdf.

Gatteschi, V., Lamberti, F., Demartini, C., Pranteda, C., & Santamaría, V. (2018). To blockchain or not to blockchain: That is the question. *IT Professional, 20*(2), 62–74. https://doi.org/10.1109/MITP.2018.021921652.

Giudici, G., & Adhami, S. (2019). The impact of governance signals on ICO fundraising success. *Journal of Industrial and Business Economics, 46*(2), 283–312.

Giudici, G., Milne, A., & Vinogradov, D. (2020). Cryptocurrencies: Market analysis and perspectives. *Journal of Industrial and Business Economics, 47*(1), 1–18.

Guo, Y., & Liang, C. (2016). Blockchain application and outlook in the banking industry. *Financial Innovation, 2*(1), 24.

Holotiuk, F., Pisani, F., & Moormann, J. (2017). *The impact of blockchain technology on business models in the payments industry*. In Proceedings of

13th International Conference on Wirtschaftsinformatik, St. Gallen, 12–15 February, pp. 912–926.

Houben, R., & Snyers, A. (2018). *Cryptocurrencies and blockchain: Legal context and implications for financial crime, money laundering and tax evasion*. European Parliament. Available at: https://www.europarl.europa.eu/cmsdata/150761/TAX3%20Study%20on%20cryptocurrencies%20and%20blockchain.pdf.

Howell, S. T., Niessner, M., & Yermack, D. (2018). *Initial coin offerings: Financing growth with cryptocurrency token sales* (No. w24774). National Bureau of Economic Research. Available at: https://www.nber.org/system/files/working_papers/w24774/w24774.pdf.

Huang, W., Meoli, M., & Vismara, S. (2019). The geography of initial coin offerings. *Small business economics*, 1–26.

Iansiti, M., & Lakhani, K. R. (2017). The truth about blockchain. *Harvard Business Review, 95*(1), 118–127.

Jacobs, G. (2018). Cryptocurrencies and the challenge of global governance. *Cadmus, 3*(4), 109–123.

Lauslahti, K., Mattila, J., & Seppala, T. (2017). Smart contracts–How will blockchain technology affect contractual practices? *Etla Reports* (68).

Lewis, R., McPartland, J., & Ranjan, R. (2017). Blockchain and financial market innovation. *Economic Perspectives, 41*(7), 1–17. Federal Reserve Bank of Chicago.

Li, W., Andreina, S., Bohli, J. M., & Karame, G. (2017). Securing proof-of-stake blockchain protocols. In *Data privacy management, cryptocurrencies and blockchain technology* (pp. 297–315). Cham: Springer.

MacDonald, T. J., Allen, D. W., & Potts, J. (2016). Blockchains and the boundaries of self-organized economies: Predictions for the future of banking. *Banking beyond banks and money* (pp. 279–296). Cham: Springer.

Martino, P. (2019). Blockchain technology: Challenges and opportunities for banks. *International Journal of Financial Innovation in Banking, 2*(4), 314–333.

Martino, P., Bellavitis, C., & DaSilva, C. M. (2020). Cryptocurrencies and entrepreneurial finance. In J. M. Munoz & M. Frenkel (Eds.), *The economics of cryptocurrencies* (pp. 51–56).

Martino, P., Wang, K. J., Bellavitis, C., & DaSilva, C. M. (2019). *An introduction to blockchain, cryptocurrency and initial coin offerings*. New frontiers in entrepreneurial finance research, 181–206.

Massey, R., Dalal, D., & Dakshinamoorthy, A. (2017). *Initial coin offering: A new paradigm*. Available at: https://www2.deloitte.com/content/dam/Deloitte/us/Documents/process-and-operations/us-cons-new-paradigm.pdf.

Nakamoto, S. (2008). *Bitcoin: A peer-to-peer electronic cash* System. Available at: https://bitcoin.org/bitcoin.pdf.

Narayanan, A., Bonneau, J., Felten, E., Miller, A., & Goldfeder, S. (2016). *Bitcoin and cryptocurrency technologies: A comprehensive introduction*. Princeton University Press.

Natarajan, H., Krause, S., & Gradstein, H. (2017). *Distributed ledger technology and blockchain*. World Bank. Available at: https://olc.worldbank.org/system/files/122140-WP-PUBLIC-Distributed-Ledger-Technology-and-Blockchain-Fintech-Notes.pdf.

Niranjanamurthy, M., Nithya, B. N., & Jagannatha, S. (2018). Analysis of blockchain technology: Pros, cons and SWOT. *Cluster Computing*, 1–15. https://doi.org/10.1007/s10586-018-2387-5.

Nofer, M., Gomber, P., Hinz, O., & Schiereck, D. (2017). Blockchain. *Business & Information Systems Engineering, 59*(3), 183–187. https://doi.org/10.1007/s12599-017-0467-3.

Nomura Research Institute. (2016). *Survey on blockchain technologies and related services*, FY2015 Report March 2016. Available at: https://www.meti.go.jp/english/press/2016/pdf/0531_01f.pdf.

Nowiński, W., & Kozma, M. (2017). How can blockchain technology disrupt the existing business models? *Entrepreneurial Business and Economics Review, 5*(3), 173–188.

OECD. (2002). *The future of money*. Available at: https://www.oecd.org/futures/35391062.pdf.

Peters, G. W., & Panayi, E. (2016). Understanding modern banking ledgers through blockchain technologies: Future of transaction processing and smart contracts on the internet of money. *Banking beyond banks and money* (pp. 239–278). Cham: Springer.

Richter, C., Kraus, S., & Bouncken, R. B. (2015). Virtual currencies like bitcoin as a paradigm shift in the field of transactions. *International Business & Economics Research Journal (IBER), 14*(4), 575–586.

Securities and Exchange Commission (SEC). (2017). *Investor bulletin: Initial coin offerings*. Available at: https://www.sec.gov/oiea/investor-alerts-and-bulletins/ib_coinofferings.

Swan, M. (2015). *Blockchain: Blueprint for a new economy, O'Reilly Media Inc, 1005 Gravenstein Highway North* (p. 95472). CA: Sebastopol.

Swanson, T. (2015). *Consensus-as-a-service: A brief report on the emergence of permissioned, distributed ledger systems*. Available at: https://www.ofnumbers.com/wp-content/uploads/2015/04/Permissioned-distributed-ledgers.pdf.

Szabo, N. (1994). Smart contracts, unpublished manuscript. Available at: https://szabo.best.vwh.net/smart.contracts.html.

Szabo, N. (1997). The idea of smart contracts. *Nick Szabo's Papers and Concise Tutorials, 6*.

Tapscott, A., & Tapscott, D. (2017). How blockchain is changing finance. *Harvard Business Review, 1*(9), 2–5.

UBS. (April 2018). *The road to cashless societies*. Available at: https://www.ubs.com/content/dam/WealthManagementAmericas/cio-impact/shifting%20in%20asia.pdf.

Walport, M. (2016). *Distributed ledger technology: Beyond blockchain*. UK Government Office for Science. Available at: https://assets.publishing.service.gov.uk/government/uploads/system/uploads/attachment_data/file/492972/gs-16-1-distributed-ledger-technology.pdf.

Wang, S., Ouyang, L., Yuan, Y., Ni, X., Han, X., & Wang, F. Y. (2019). Blockchain-enabled smart contracts: Architecture, applications, and future trends. *IEEE Transactions on Systems, Man, and Cybernetics: Systems, 49*(11), 2266–2277.

Yermack, D. (2013). Is Bitcoin a real currency? An economic appraisal (No. w19747). *National Bureau of Economic Research, 2013*. Available at: https://www.nber.org/system/files/working_papers/w19747/w19747.pdf.

Yermack, D. (2017). Corporate governance and blockchains. *Review of Finance, 21*(1), 7–31.

Zheng, Z., Xie, S., Dai, H., Chen, X., & Wang, H. (2017). *An overview of blockchain technology: Architecture, consensus, and future trends*. In IEEE International Congress on Big Data (BigData Congress), IEEE, pp. 557–564.

Zheng, Z., Xie, S., Dai, H. N., Chen, X., & Wang, H. (2018). Blockchain challenges and opportunities: A survey. *International Journal of Web and Grid Services, 14*(4), 352–375.

CHAPTER 3

Blockchain Technology and the Banking Industry

Abstract Blockchain technology has been widely acknowledged as a disruptive force in the financial sector that is capable of undermining traditional business models and the technologies currently in use in many financial service transactions. This chapter focuses on blockchain technology's potential implications for the banking industry. Building on the results of a previous study that I conducted through qualitative-based interviews with three professional bankers from different European banks tackling the challenges of blockchain, this chapter discusses the potential advantages and risks that blockchain technology poses to banks and identifies the main banking areas that can be affected.

Keywords Blockchain · Banking competition · Banking efficiency · Financial inclusion · Product innovation

3.1 Introduction

Blockchain technology—along with its main applications, namely cryptocurrencies and smart contracts—has attracted a great deal of attention and stimulated rich discussions among academics, practitioners and regulators around the world. It is now acknowledged as a disruptive force in the financial sector and can undermine the traditional business models

P. Martino, *Blockchain and Banking*,
https://doi.org/10.1007/978-3-030-70970-9_3

and technologies that are currently employed in many key financial service transactions. As Philippon (2016, p. 2) notes, "such innovations can disrupt existing industry structures and blur industry boundaries, facilitate strategic disintermediation, revolutionize how existing firms create and deliver products and services, provide new gateways for entrepreneurship, democratize access to financial services, but also create significant privacy, regulatory and law enforcement challenges".

Regarding the banking industry in particular, the growing interest in blockchain technology results from its ability to create new opportunities for banks and to pose new threats to their business, as it may improve the efficiency of the processes underlying the financial services offer, thereby fostering the offer of higher-quality services. It may also allow the entry of new operators with a consequent expansion of the competitive context. However, like any emerging technology, blockchain's potential implications are both far-reaching and not yet fully understood.

To shed light on the implications of blockchain technology in the banking sector, this chapter seeks to explain (1) the potential benefits, as well as risks, that blockchain may pose for banks and (2) the main banking areas that may be affected by the adoption of this technology. The chapter is based on the results of a previous study I conducted through qualitative-based interviews with three professional bankers in different European banks that are dealing with the challenges of blockchain[1]. The study was published in the *International Journal of Financial Innovation in Banking* in 2019.[2]

3.2 Blockchain as a Potential Risk for Banks

With regard to blockchain's potential implications for banks, it is worth noting that the first-generation blockchain (Blockchain 1.0.)—that is, blockchain used to support Bitcoin (and other cryptocurrencies)[3]—was

[1] The actors interviewed are two general managers and the chief innovation officer of three medium to large international banks located in Switzerland, the UK and Italy.

[2] Martino, P. (2019). Blockchain technology: challenges and opportunities for banks. *International Journal of Financial Innovation in Banking*, *2*(4), 314–333. https://dx.doi.org/10.1504/IJFIB.2019.104535. Inderscience Enterprises Ltd. retains the copyright of the original article.

[3] The reference in this paragraph is to public or permissionless blockchains, where Bitcoin and other cryptocurrencies typically operate.

initially designed as a platform for disintermediation (Martino 2019). Its main purpose was to create an electronic payment system to allow the direct transfer of value between two parties without the need for a trusted third party (a central authority or an intermediary like a bank). Disintermediation means the blockchain linked to cryptocurrencies eliminates the need for intermediaries such as banks because it enables individuals and organisations to transact and forge agreements directly with one another without risks. In this way, banks are no longer needed to verify the parties' identities, establish trust or perform critical activities like the contracting, clearing, settling and record-keeping of tasks (McDonald et al. 2016; Holotiuk et al. 2017; Iansiti and Lakhani 2017).

In theory, first-generation blockchain poses a threat to the banking industry since blockchain and Bitcoin (as well as other cryptocurrencies), taken together, are tools for disintermediating banks. According to McDonald et al. (2016), blockchain can be considered a new institutional technology that might re-order the governance of the production of banking services since it enables bank transactions to move away from centralised hierarchical organisations towards a decentralised market.

Today, transferring value in a final way requires a long process with numerous players (e.g. customers, banks, clearing systems, settlement systems and so on) working on a SWIFT network,[4] which banks use to transfer all types of financial information. To move money effectively, several centralised systems act as a "notary" of the transaction, making it a very long and complex process. Via blockchain, in conjunction with Bitcoin (and other cryptocurrencies), this process can take place in a direct, secure and "final" way without the involvement of the players mentioned above. Specifically, owing to the key characteristics of the distributed ledger technology (see Chapter 2), blockchain linked to cryptocurrencies makes it possible for two people who do not know each other to directly exchange digital assets in a secure and "final" way. This means that, at the end of the transaction, there is an effective ownership transfer (Martino 2019).

Based on the considerations above, first-generation blockchain can be considered a new player that competes with banks, since blockchain and

[4]The Society for Worldwide Interbank Financial Telecommunication (SWIFT) is an international telematic communication network between the financial institutions associated with it. It allows financial institutions worldwide to send and receive information about financial transactions in a secure, standardised and reliable environment.

cryptocurrencies facilitate new tools that can be deployed to manage the difficulties of transacting (MacDonald et al. 2016; Lindman et al. 2017; Frame et al. 2018), and they offer significant advantages over banks in several areas (e.g. payments) by allowing a fast, low-cost and secure way to transfer value. These advantages, as explained above, are associated with the elimination of intermediaries in transactions and the consequent banking fees. Furthermore, new blockchain-based start-ups (i.e. so-called fintech companies) may emerge and offer some banking services with lower fees, thus potentially causing banks to lose their market share (Philippon 2016; Stulz 2019). For instance, many fintech start-ups are active today in segments of the value chain that are already managed by banks, such as business and consumer lending (PwC 2020). Such firms leverage blockchain technology to offer credits and funding to individuals and businesses with lower transaction costs; thus, they compete with traditional commercial banks. In this way, blockchain and cryptocurrencies may jeopardise one of the banking sector's core business activities (i.e. lending), with the consequent erosion of bank revenue, thus undermining the banks' profitability (Yeoh 2017). According to Gartner (2018), one of the world's leading research and advisory companies, 80% of heritage financial services firms will go out of business by 2030, become commoditised or exist only formally without competing effectively. The reason for this is that global digital platforms, fintech companies and other players will gain greater market share by using emerging technologies, such as blockchain, to change the industry's economic and business models.

Today, the largest banks acknowledge the potential risks posed by this new competitor. In its annual 10-K filing with the Securities and Exchange Commission (SEC) released in February 2019, the Bank of America Corporation (BofA) listed cryptocurrencies among the risk factors that could have an impact on the bank's competitiveness and reduce its revenues and profits. BofA reported that technological advances (such as cryptocurrencies) have enabled new players to offer products and services that had traditionally been banking products, as well as new innovative products, at a lower price, thereby increasing competition, which, in turn, may harm bank earnings through several channels. For instance, BofA points out that these new technologies create pressure on banks to lower the prices of—or the credit standards applied to—their products and services, require substantial expenditures to modify or adapt existing products and services in order to stay competitive and affect the willingness of customers to do business with banks. This can reduce banks' net interest margin and revenues from their fee-based products and services. This view is also supported by the large US bank JPMorgan Chase, which acknowledged in its annual 10-K filing that payment processing and other banking services could be significantly disrupted by new technologies like cryptocurrencies. It pointed out how these technologies require that banks make additional investments for them to remain competitive and can put pressure on the pricing of banks' products and services or cause the bank to lose market share, particularly as far as traditional banking products like deposits and bank accounts are concerned. According to JPMorgan Chase, any such impact could reduce the bank's revenues and profitability.

Nonetheless, the potential risks mentioned above do not pose an immediate threat to banks, since the application of blockchain linked to cryptocurrencies is constrained by several limitations: there are numerous regulatory issues (linked to illicit activities like money laundering, terrorist financing and tax evasion), technical/scalability problems, business model challenges, government rules and others that currently limit the use of this kind of blockchain and mitigate the associated risks for banks (Martino 2019).

Regulation issues are among the most important problems limiting the application of blockchain linked to cryptocurrencies at present since the banking sector is highly regulated, while blockchain and cryptocurrencies are, for the most part, not (yet). For instance, for issues related to terrorism and tax avoidance, among others, banks must track transactions step by step, which is not always feasible with first-generation blockchain, thus raising issues related to transaction traceability. As Houben and Snyers (2018) argue, cryptocurrencies are thought to be very suitable for illicit activities given their anonymity, cross-border nature and quick transferability. The anonymity, in particular, which can vary from complete anonymity to pseudo-anonymity, prevents cryptocurrency transactions from being adequately monitored, thus allowing transactions to occur outside the regulatory perimeter and, consequently, enabling individuals to use cryptocurrencies for their unlawful actions. Therefore, regulators around the world are worried about criminals increasingly using cryptocurrencies to commit fraud and manipulation, tax evasion, hacking and money laundering or to fund terrorist activities, and they are trying to overcome such problems by regulating cryptocurrencies (see Chapter 5). Another set of issues relates to privacy: in a simple transaction between two subjects, only the parties that participated in the operation (e.g.

customers, banks, the central bank and the clearing system) have access to information about the transaction; by contrast, with public blockchain, everyone can access this information and see that one person has sent money to another. Also, as explained in Chapter 2, the transparency inherent in public blockchain is such that anyone can retrieve the history of all transactions performed on a blockchain and rely on big data analytics to retrieve potentially sensitive information (De Filippi 2016). These regulatory problems currently limit the application of blockchain linked to cryptocurrencies as a potential competitor to banks in areas like payment and lending. This, in turn, reduces the resulting risks to banks' core business and profitability.

Finally, other problems that limit the use of blockchain linked to cryptocurrencies and, consequently, reduce the potential risks for banks concern scalability and the high volatility of Bitcoin and other cryptocurrencies. Regarding scalability problems, as explained in Chapter 2, public blockchain on which cryptocurrencies operate can process only four to seven operations per second, while traditional systems today carry out even thousands of operations per second, thus making the latter more convenient than blockchain. The high volatility of cryptocurrencies generates problems relating to exchange rates with fiat currencies and the consequent foreign exchange risks.

Owing to these limitations today, it is difficult to view blockchain linked to cryptocurrencies as a competitor to banks in areas such as payment and lending, although it does represent a threat that will likely become more significant in the future, particularly if banks fail to fully exploit their potential and end up leaving room for new competitors.

3.3 Blockchain and Banking Efficiency

While banks are wary of using blockchain technology linked to cryptocurrencies (first-generation blockchain) because of the lack of regulation and technical problems, they are embracing blockchain's underlying distributed ledger technology, particularly private or permissioned blockchain,[5] thanks to the many benefits it may offer. As explained in the previous chapter, since a permissioned blockchain is a closed system between pre-defined organisations, it does not suffer from public

[5] The reference here is to second-generation blockchains (particularly private blockchains).

blockchain's regulatory issues (e.g. traceability and privacy issues). Also, it requires lower costs and computational power to work than public blockchains, thus mitigating scalability concerns.

By exploiting the "good side" of blockchain (i.e. the fact that the information is distributed and shared only among those with permission and in an immutable way, guaranteeing cybersecurity), banks may obtain several advantages. Many scholars and financial players (Buitenhek 2016; Guo and Liang 2016; Peters and Panayi 2016) suggest that the distributed ledger technology of blockchain may solve most of the problems currently affecting traditional banking processes, such as efficiency bottlenecks, transaction lags, fraud and operational risks, by cutting costs, boosting process efficiency and increasing security. According to these studies, blockchain may be applied to change the ways financial services are offered and will improve traditional financial institutions' competitive advantages by enabling smart contracts, maintaining immutable logs of transactions and facilitating the real-time execution of transactions (McKinsey & Company 2016; KPMG 2017).

Hence, if banks can integrate blockchain's distributed ledger technology into their business model to provide their services, they may exploit its benefits to improve their efficiency in terms of reducing operational cost and time. Specifically, blockchain has the potential to reshape traditional banking processes, which can help banks to automate inter-organisational processes, improve transparency and reset existing operational benchmarks.

There are numerous areas of application for blockchain technology, and they concern different banking processes and operations (Yermack 2019). According to a study by Santander InnoVentures (the Spanish bank's fintech investment arm), in collaboration with Oliver Wyman and the Anthemis Group (2015), it is possible to identify 20–25 usage cases where blockchain technology may be applied. The study also estimates that blockchain's distributed ledger technology could cut banks' infrastructure costs by up to between $15 billion and $20 billion a year by 2022. These usage cases include several banking areas and operations such as international money transfers, trade finance, syndicated lending, securities trading and regulatory compliance. In line with these findings, a joint analysis by Accenture and McLagen (2017) estimates that blockchain may reduce infrastructure costs for eight of the world's 10 largest investment banks by an average of 30%, which means $8 billion to $12 billion in annual cost savings for those banks, including: a 70% reduction in central financial reporting; a 30% to 50% reduction in compliance; a 50% reduction in centralised operations such as know-your-customer (KYC) operations and client on-boarding; and a 50% reduction in business operations such as trade support, clearance and settlement.

As I will discuss below, any banking area characterised by long processes, multiple handovers, a lot of paperwork across industries, many involved parties and where access to information is relevant may generally benefit from the adoption of blockchain technology to improve operations and boost efficiency (Buitenhek 2016; Guo and Liang 2016; Peters and Panayi 2016; Casey et al. 2018; Martino 2019).

3.3.1 Loans and Capital Markets

An oft-suggested example of where blockchain can be applied to improve process efficiency are clearing and settlement systems, which currently require a complex process with many players, myriad messages and manual reconciliations and are, therefore, characterised by long times (Buithenek 2016; Fanning and Centers 2016; Peters and Panayi 2016). Blockchain technology may provide a better clearing and settlement system by allowing banks to clear and settle directly and securely, thereby reducing operational costs and timing for activities like corporate lending and capital markets. According to an Accenture Consulting (2017) study, large investment banks could save $10 billion by using blockchain technology to improve the efficiency of clearing and settlement, which are currently managed via a host of messages and manual reconciliations.

Thus, activities such as securities transactions, where post-trade clearing and settlement is slow and expensive and involves many parties, may benefit from the adoption of blockchain (Yermack 2019), which can securely and transparently move securities in seconds or minutes, with automatic clearing and settlement (Buithenek 2016). As a consequence, this would lead to reduced costs and lower counterparty risk associated with clearing and settlement (McKinsey & Company 2016). Several transactions have demonstrated the blockchain's impact on capital markets. For instance, in April 2019, Société Générale SFH, a subsidiary of Société Générale Group, issued €100 million in covered bonds as a security token directly registered on the Ethereum blockchain, exploring a more efficient process for bond issuances by reducing costs and the number of intermediaries involved. Subsequently, in September 2019, Banco Santander issued the first end-to-end blockchain bond (worth $20 million) using the public Ethereum blockchain, which allowed the bank to tokenise the bond securely (i.e. digitally represent traditional assets on the blockchain) and register it in a permissioned manner on the blockchain. The automation of the entire process enabled the bank to reduce the number of intermediaries required in the process, making the transaction faster, simpler and more efficient.

Another activity in this area covers syndicated loans, which take on average around 20 days for a transaction to be settled by the banks due to the quantity of information exchanged, lengthy reviews and the paper forms of communication between parties (Fanning and Centers 2016). Blockchain may reduce the time and costs for the transaction by automating the entire process and making it more transparent. First, when a party enters contract information into the blockchain, information is made available in real time to all other parties, thus removing the need for paper communications and multiple contract reviews. Also, smart contracts can be used to digitise the syndicated loan to reconcile trades against credit agreements, automatically debit interest payments from the borrower's account and adjust loan liability within the blockchain. As Rutenberg and Wenner (2017) suggest, by using smart contacts, it is possible to manage the entire process—from entering into the loan contract and collecting interest payments to calling a default and even seizing collateral—without any human involvement. This can reduce the need for manual reconciliations and processing, which can result in time and cost savings. For instance, in 2018, Spain's BBVA and two partner banks (MUFG of Japan and BNP Paribas of France) completed the first syndicated loan (to the tune of €150 million) on blockchain with the Red Eléctrica corporation, thus providing a working example of how such transactions can be simplified and accelerated by using blockchain technology. The whole negotiation process was done over a private blockchain network, which significantly expedited the process while ensuring full documentation tracking and negotiation transparency.

3.3.2 *Trade Finance*

Blockchain may also positively affect trade finance, a business area characterised by high costs and low efficiency because many processes involve extensive manual inspections, paper-based transactions (e.g. letters of credit) and numerous intermediaries.

Friction in global markets makes obtaining financing and completing trades a lengthy and complex process that includes various activities such as lending, issuing letters of credit, factoring and insuring the parties (Lang 2017). Financial institutions are required to make credit assessments and perform payments—often through paper-based exchange and validation of documents—across multiple participants (FBS 2019). In general, it can take days to weeks to complete a single transaction.

Blockchain technology can help to alleviate these frictions in trade by reducing the extensive amount of documentation and complex document flows involved (Cong and He 2019; Yermack 2019). By using blockchain technology to digitalise and authenticate records (e.g. via smart contracts) and allowing the parties involved in an operation to access the same information, it is possible to reduce time, cost and operational risk (Buithenek 2016; Guo and Liang 2016). This means that blockchain may enable participants from different sectors (e.g. banking and freight shipping) to directly interact and share information in a more easily verifiable and decentralised manner to increase the speed of transactions and reduce the need for paper reconciliation (FSB 2019). For instance, in May 2018, HSBC and ING Bank completed the world's first commercially viable trade finance transaction for the international food and agriculture conglomerate Cargill by using blockchain (specifically, R3's scalable Corda blockchain platform). HSBC issued a letter of credit to ING for the firm Cargill and executed the transaction in a record time of 24 hours instead of the standard period of 5–10 days by removing the need for paper reconciliation, since all parties were linked on the platform and updated instantaneously.

3.3.3 Payment Systems

Another banking area that could benefit from the adoption of blockchain technologies covers payments systems, which would mean shifting parts of banks' payment systems to blockchain technology so that it may facilitate faster payments at lower costs. Currently, value transfer is expensive and slow, particularly in cross-border payments, because of a series of complicated processes (e.g. manual reconciliation) and the need for intermediary clearing firms. A single payment transaction often involves a significant number of parties and is typically carried out through decentralised and complex correspondent banking networks that face challenges relating to cost and customer due diligence, as well as inefficiencies from operations across different currencies, message formats, time zones and laws (FSB 2019). For example, sending $100 from a country in Europe to a country in Africa can cost around $10 extra and require several (on average, five) days for processing.

Blockchain technology may make it possible to accept payments instantly and reduce transaction inefficiency by automating reconciliation, reducing operational costs or increasing the availability of "know-your-customer" (KYC) data. Specifically, by applying blockchain technology to payments, transactions can be executed directly between banks without any third party, thus simplifying the process and offering many advantages to banks, such as lower transaction and operational costs, as well as increased processing speed (Buithenek 2016; Fanning and Centers 2016; Guo and Liang 2016). According to estimates by Deloitte (2016), business-to-business and person-to-person payments across borders with blockchain may result in a 40–80% reduction in transaction costs and take an average of four to six seconds to finalise, instead of the standard transfer process of two to three days. In April 2018, Banco Santander launched the first blockchain-based international money transfer service, which makes it possible for customers to complete international transfers on the same day or by the next day. It also shows the exact amount that customers will receive in the destination currency before they make the transfer.

3.3.4 Compliance

By automating parts of banks' business processes, blockchain may also significantly reduce the costs associated with areas like compliance, which are characterised by highly manual and paper-based processes that lead to delays, inefficiencies and increased exposure to errors and fraud (Capgemini Consulting 2016).

The burden of providing regulators with more and more data around the world is a time-consuming task for the financial institutions and regulators who have to process such vast amounts of information. Blockchain could significantly reduce the costs associated with such operations. It may simplify all administrative work involved in the compliance process since with blockchain a transaction is automatic, and then it automatically feeds the compliance database. For instance, Buithenek (2016) suggests that blockchain, by enabling smart contracts, could make it possible to enforce compliance upfront instead of verifying it after a transaction, thereby dramatically reducing the time and effort that financial institutions spend on regulatory reporting and improving the quality, accuracy and speed of the entire process. As a result, it will also reduce the costs involved. This means that compliance can work in real time concerning the payment process (and, in general, any banking activity), improve the speed of processes and reduce the related costs. Furthermore, blockchain may be used to keep track of the steps that regulations require: immutably recording transactions on the distributed ledger, which renders information decentralised and accessible, provides a comprehensive, secure and irreversible financial audit trail for regulators to verify compliance, thus eliminating the need for regulators to collect, store, reconcile and aggregate information. By allowing regulators and central banks to independently extract information on transactions, banks may avoid all the administrative work, which reduces the need to actively collect, verify and deliver data (e.g. sending thousands of reports) (Auer 2019).

3.3.5 Know Your Customer

Using blockchain to share information about customers may also improve the efficiency of know-your-customer (KYC) processes by reducing the unnecessary duplication of information and requests (Lang 2017; Moyano and Ross 2017).

The KYC process consists of an exchange of documents between the customer and the financial institution to collect customers' basic identity information (Moyano and Ross 2017). Such processes in many financial institutions are inefficient and characterised by long times, the duplication of effort and a potential for error, which are costly and could also harm customers' experience (Capgemini 2019). A global survey by Thomson Reuters (2016) reports that the costs and complexity of KYC are rising, and financial institutions are spending between $60 million and $500 million per year to keep up with KYC and customer due diligence regulations.

Blockchain's distributed ledger technology can speed up the KYC process and make it more secure and efficient. Through its cryptographic protection, which helps to keep information secure, and its ability to share a constantly updated record with many parties, blockchain may ensure consistent and reliable customer information. This means that once customers carry out the full KYC process with one bank, information resulting from the KYC process may be shared with other banks, which will eliminate redundant work and reduce the number of steps in current KYC practices. Fundamentally, blockchain may enable the creation of a chronological, decentralised and shared data depository in which banks that need to conduct KYC practices for a customer can directly verify the result of the process that has already been conducted for this customer, thereby avoiding duplicate KYC tasks and achieving cost and time savings. This may lead to an increase in efficiency in the broad sense, both as lower costs and time to do KYC processes and because the customer has the immediate benefit of opening an account, unlike other current systems. Indeed, from a customer standpoint, blockchain can reduce on-boarding wait times and eliminate the need to repeatedly provide the same information to their financial services providers (KPMG 2018).

Taken together, the considerations above are particularly interesting in terms of banks' potential profitability. If banks can incorporate this technology into their business models and boost their efficiency in terms of cost reductions, they may reduce the commissions they charge their customers and have a better margin, since the decrease in the commissions may be balanced by the decrease in costs. Thus, blockchain can be instrumental in improving the quality of the services offered to clients, which will provide an important competitive edge. Nonetheless, it is worth noting that, to date, there has not been any evidence of blockchain technology usage leading to efficiency improvements (i.e. cost reductions). It will take two to three years before blockchain proves that it works effectively and can generate advantages for banks (Martino 2019).

Furthermore, several issues must be addressed before blockchain may reveal all the benefits mentioned above. For instance, regarding the benefits identified in compliance processes (the KYC process and regulatory reporting), there are regulatory issues (e.g. relating to privacy and security, like the General Data Protection Regulation or GDPR[6]) that may constrain the use of blockchain technology in these banking processes. In KYC processes, for example, privacy issues must be addressed before adopting blockchain, since customers must first authorise the sharing of their data between banks. Thus, it is necessary to address these issues before adopting blockchain in these areas. Moreover, there is the problem

[6]The GDPR (General Data Protection Regulation) aims to create a harmonised data protection law across the European Union and allowing users to take back control of their personal data.

of the progressive adoption of blockchain and the resulting standardisation to allow for interoperability, that is, the ability to share information without restrictions across different blockchain networks (Casey et al. 2018). Specifically, different blockchain systems will need to be interoperable with other ledgers and integrated with existing systems if they are to be introduced at scale into the financial system. As research by Moody's (2019) suggests, standardisation is vital to improving interoperability between blockchains, applications built on the same blockchain, and between blockchains and legacy IT systems, thereby facilitating the establishment of blockchain-based ecosystems. This means that the involvement of the entire banking system is essential: it becomes profitable to use blockchain only if all banks adopt the same methodology to transmit information. Then, it is necessary to have collaboration across industries (i.e. other financial institutions, such as insurance or non-financial companies) and along the value chain to enable the broad adoption of blockchain and harness its benefits.

3.4 Blockchain as a Source for New Products and Services

In addition to improvements in banking processes' efficiency, a further benefit of blockchain for banks is access to lots of information. Having recorded on the distributed ledger a full and transparent history that any client banks have on board, blockchain may provide a way for banks to gain swift and secure access to updated customer data, resulting in greater operational efficiency and a reduction in the time and cost needed to gather and process data.

Data is a key source to build up information that can provide the firm with a competitive advantage (Prescott 2016). Since information on customer payments and credit profiles represents a source of knowledge about customers for banks, banks may utilise this information as a key resource to generate new products and services in order to better address customer needs (Martino 2019). Nevertheless, the key advantage for banks is the ability to access numerous and diversified kinds of information—relating not only to the bank (e.g. information on customers) but also to other organisations such as ships, ports and so on and their resulting exploitation—to create new products and services that do not exist yet. The availability of a series of distributed information derived from a variety of sources gives banks a better and more complete understanding of their customers' behaviours, needs and preferences (Prescott 2016), which enables banks to create and offer products and services tailored to these customers' individual needs.

Hence, creating new products and services by utilising information on the blockchain may generate major new revenue streams for banks and may be key to gaining a competitive edge (Vermeulen 2004; Accenture 2016).

3.5 Blockchain and Financial Inclusion

About 1.7 billion individuals today do not have an account with a financial institution (Demirguc-Kunt et al. 2018). They constitute what has been called the unbanked population, while many other individuals have limited access to traditional financial services and are known as the underbanked population.[7] Together, these groups account for some 2 billion financially excluded individuals worldwide.[8] Moreover, over half the micro, small and mid-sized enterprises (MSMEs) in emerging markets, equalling more than 200 million businesses, currently do not have access to banking services (EY 2017).

These individuals face difficulties accessing banking services for several reasons. First, banks have difficulties reaching these individuals because of their poor credit histories and the lack of appropriate identification needed to open a bank account, for example, which makes it hard to implement KYC practices and other eligibility and due diligence requirements to formally open an account. Additional problems relate to the affordability of financial products and services, deficient payment and credit infrastructures, the limited geographical access to financial institutions and so on (Natarajan et al. 2017; Lichtfous et al. 2018).

New technologies can facilitate more efficient access to this market, effectively making the costs and profits in serving this segment more attractive (Ouma et al. 2017; EY 2017). This part of the world population may represent a key opportunity for banks since blockchain technology could allow them to access banking services much more easily.

[7] For example, they use money orders, cheque-cashing services and other instruments offered through providers other than traditional financial institutions.

[8] The majority of this population is found in low- and middle-income emerging markets.

Thus, with blockchain, banks may reach unbanked and underbanked individuals by addressing their needs and solving most of the abovementioned challenges (Natarajan et al. 2017; Lichtfous et al. 2018; Schuetz and Venkatesh 2020). First, banks can reach these individuals by allowing them to create their own financial alternatives (e.g. cryptocurrencies) that meet specific customer needs at an affordable cost (EY 2017). The advantage can stem from using the digital currency as the transfer medium between two parties globally (i.e. as a universal means of exchange), which lowers transaction costs by preventing individuals from paying currency fees when they transfer money to different countries. Since they are universal currencies, cryptocurrencies eliminate the foreign exchange transaction fees that banks usually charge. Second, owing to the technology's ability to establish a digital identity rapidly and cost-effectively, blockchain may enable banks to solve problems linked to KYC processes when trying to serve these potential customers, thus allowing the financial inclusion of previously underserved consumer segments.

These considerations suggest that blockchain may open new market segments for existing banks and allow them to reach many new potential customers, thereby generating new revenue streams and improving their profitability. According to Accenture (2015) estimates, by bringing today's excluded individuals and businesses—particularly those in the larger and more affluent emerging market regions—into the formal banking sector banks could generate about $380 billion annually in new revenues. This view is also supported by recent research conducted by EY (2017), which indicates that banks can drive inclusive growth, restore trust and boost profits by serving underbanked individuals and businesses in emerging markets. Specifically, EY (2017) estimates that banks could generate incremental annual revenue of $200 billion by better serving financially excluded individuals and MSMEs in 60 emerging countries.

3.6 Conclusions

This chapter shed light on blockchain's potential implications for banks. It is important to differentiate between blockchain technology linked to cryptocurrencies (i.e. first-generation blockchain) and blockchain's distributed ledger technology (i.e. second-generation blockchain). While blockchain linked to cryptocurrencies is perceived as a potential threat to banks because blockchain and cryptocurrencies represent a tool to disintermediate banks, blockchain's distributed ledger technology (particularly private or permissioned blockchain) provides an opportunity since it may improve banking processes' efficiency and the services that banks offer to their customers, with a positive impact on banks' profitability. Lending, payment systems, trade finance and capital market are the main banking areas that could benefit from adopting blockchain technology. Moreover, blockchain may enable banks to create new product and services and to reach new customers from among the unbanked and underbanked populations, thus potentially generating major new revenue streams.

Although blockchain is two-sided, it currently presents an opportunity for rather than a risk to banks because the use of blockchain linked to cryptocurrencies is hampered by several regulatory and technical issues that currently reduce the potential risks to banks. Conversely, banks can exploit the benefits of blockchain's distributed ledger technology by incorporating the technology into their business models.

References

Accenture. (2015). *Billion reasons to bank inclusively*. Available at: https://www.accenture.com/us-en/_acnmedia/Accenture/Conversion-Assets/DotCom/Documents/Global/PDF/Dualpub_22/Accenture-billion-reasons-bank-inclusively.pdf.

Accenture. (2016). *Blockchain technology: How banks are building a real-time global payment network*. Available at: https://www.accenture.com/t00010101T000000Z__w__/fr-fr/_acnmedia/PDF-35/Accenture-Blockchain-How-Banks-Building-Real-Time-Global-Payment-Network.PDFla%3Dfr-FR%23zoom%3D50.

Accenture Consulting. (2017). *Banking on blockchain. A value analysis for investment banks*, Technical Report. Available at: https://www.accenture.com/us-en/insight-banking-on-blockchain.

Auer, R. (2019). *Embedded supervision: How to build regulation into blockchain finance*. BIS Working Papers No 811. Available at: https://www.bis.org/publ/work811.pdf.

Buitenhek, M. (2016). Understanding and applying blockchain technology in banking: Evolution or revolution? *Journal of Digital Banking*, *1*(2), 111–119.

Capgemini. (2019). *Banks can mitigate know-your-customer pain points with distributed ledger technology*. Available at: https://www.capgemini.com/dk-en/2019/11/banks-can-mitigate-know-your-customer-pain-points-with-distributed-ledger-technology/.

Capgemini Consulting. (2016). *Smart contracts in financial services: Getting from hype to reality*, Technical Report. Available at: https://www.capgemini.com/consulting/wp-content/uploads/sites/30/2017/07/smart-contracts.pdf.

Casey, M., Crane, J., Gensler, G., Johnson, S., & Narula, N. (2018). *The impact of blockchain technology on finance: A catalyst for change*. Geneva Reports on the World Economy 21. International Center for Monetary and Banking Studies.

Cong, L. W., & He, Z. (2019). Blockchain disruption and smart contracts. *The Review of Financial Studies, 32*(5), 1754–1797.

De Filippi, P. (2016). The interplay between decentralization and privacy: The case of blockchain technologies. *Journal of Peer Production*, (7).

Deloitte. (2016). *Cross-border payments on blockchain*. Available at: https://www2.deloitte.com/content/dam/Deloitte/global/Documents/grid/cross-border-payments.pdf.

Demirguc-Kunt, A., Klapper, L., Singer, D., Ansar, S., & Hess, J. (2018). *The global findex database 2017: Measuring financial inclusion and the fintech revolution*. The World Bank.

EY. (2017). *Innovation in financial inclusion Revenue growth through innovative inclusion*.

Fanning, K., & Centers, D. P. (2016). Blockchain and its coming impact on financial services. *Journal of Corporate Accounting and Finance, 27*(5), 53–57.

Frame, W. S., Wall, L. D., & White, L. J. (2018). *Technological change and financial innovation in banking: Some implications for fintech*. Working Paper No. 2018–11, FRB Atlanta. Available at: https://www.frbatlanta.org/-/media/documents/research/publications/wp/2018/11-technological-change-and-financial-innovation-in-banking-some-implications-for-fintech-2018-10-02.pdf.

FSB. (2019). *Decentralised financial technologies. Report on financial stability, regulatory and governance implications*. Available at: https://www.fsb.org/wp-content/uploads/P060619.pdf.

Gartner. (2018). *Digitalization will make most heritage financial firms irrelevant*. Available at: https://www.gartner.com/en/newsroom/press-releases/2018-10-29-gartner-says-digitalization-will-make-most-heritage-financial-firms-irrelevant-by-2030.

Guo, Y., & Liang, C. (2016). Blockchain application and outlook in the banking industry. *Financial Innovation, 2*(1), 24.

Holotiuk, F., Pisani, F., & Moormann, J. (2017). *The impact of blockchain technology on business models in the payments industry*. In Proceedings of 13th International Conference on Wirtschaftsinformatik, St. Gallen, 12–15 February, pp. 912–926.

Houben, R., & Snyers, A. (2018). *Cryptocurrencies and blockchain: Legal context and implications for financial crime, money laundering and tax evasion*. European Parliament. Available at: https://www.europarl.europa.eu/cmsdata/150761/TAX3%20Study%20on%20cryptocurrencies%20and%20blockchain.pdf.

Iansiti, M., & Lakhani, K. R. (2017). The truth about blockchain. *Harvard Business Review, 95*(1), 118–127.

KPMG. (2017). *Blockchain in financial services: A threat or an opportunity*. Available at: https://home.kpmg.com/ng/en/home/insights/2017/06/blockchain-in-financial-services–athreat-or-an-opportunity.html.

KPMG. (2018). *Could blockchain bethe foundation of a viable KYC utility?* Available at: https://assets.kpmg/content/dam/kpmg/xx/pdf/2018/03/kpmg-blockchain-kyc-utility.pdf.

Lang, J. (2017). *Blockchain in financial services. Three uses for blockchain in banking*. Blockchain Unleashed: IBM Blockchain Blog. Available at: https://www.ibm.com/blogs/blockchain/2017/10/three-uses-for-blockchain-in-banking.

Lichtfous, M., Yadav, V., & Fratino, V. (2018). Can blockchain accelerate financial inclusion globally. *Deloitte Inside Magazine* (19). Available at: https://www2.deloitte.com/content/dam/Deloitte/lu/Documents/technology/lu-blockchain-accelerate-financial-inclusion.pdf.

Lindman, J., Tuunainen, V. K., & Rossi, M. (2017). *Opportunities and risks of blockchain technologies—A research agenda*, in Hawaii International Conference on System Sciences (HICSS). Available at: http://hdl.handle.net/10125/41338.

MacDonald, T. J., Allen, D. W., & Potts, J. (2016). Blockchains and the boundaries of self-organized economies: Predictions for the future of banking. *Banking Beyond Banks and Money* (pp. 279–296). Cham: Springer.

Martino, P. (2019). Blockchain technology: Challenges and opportunities for banks. *International Journal of Financial Innovation in Banking, 2*(4), 314–333.

McKinsey & Company. (2016). *How blockchains could change the world*. Available at: https://www.mckinsey.com/industries/high-tech/our-insights/how-blockchains-could-changethe-world.

Moody's. (2019). *Blockchain standardisation will amplify benefits for securitisations*. Available at: https://www.moodys.com/research/Moodys-Blockchain-standardisation-will-amplify-benefits-for-securitisations–PBS_1193318?stop_mobi=yes#:~:text=Blockchain%20standards%20likely%20to%20emerge,in%20a%20report%20published%20today.

Moyano, J. P., & Ross, O. (2017). KYC optimization using distributed ledger technology. *Business & Information Systems Engineering, 59*(6), 411–423.

Natarajan, H., Krause, S., & Gradstein, H. (2017). *Distributed ledger technology and blockchain*. World Bank. Available at: https://olc.worldbank.org/system/files/122140-WP-PUBLIC-Distributed-Ledger-Technology-and-Blockchain-Fintech-Notes.pdf.

Ouma, S. A., Odongo, T. M., & Were, M. (2017). Mobile financial services and financial inclusion: Is it a boon for savings mobilization? *Review of Development Finance, 7*(1), 29–35.

Peters, G. W., & Panayi, E. (2016). Understanding modern banking ledgers through blockchain technologies: Future of transaction processing and smart contracts on the internet of money. *Banking Beyond Banks and Money* (pp. 239–278). Cham: Springer.

Philippon, T. (2016). *The fintech opportunity*. National Bureau of Economic Research Working Paper No. 22476. Available at: http://www.nber.org/papers/w22476.pdf.

Prescott, M. E. (2016). Big data: Innovation and competitive advantage in an information media analytics company. *Journal of Innovation Management, 4*(1), 92–113.

PwC. (2020). *FinTech calls for fuel to exploit a great, maturing and increasing potential*. Available at: https://www.pwc.com/it/it/industries/fintech/docs/PwC-FinTech-2020.pdf.

Rutenberg, S.A., & Wenner, R. W. (2017). *Blockchain technology: A syndicated loan revolution?* Financial Technology (FinTech) and Regulation. Available at: https://sftp.polsinelli.com/ublications/fintech/resources/upd0717fin.pdf.

Santander InnoVentures, Oliver Wyman and Anthemis Group. (2015). *The fintech 2.0 paper: Rebooting financial services*. Available at: https://www.finextra.com/finextra-downloads/newsdocs/the%20fintech%202%200%20paper.pdf.

Schuetz, S., & Venkatesh, V. (2020). Blockchain, adoption, and financial inclusion in India: Research opportunities. *International Journal of Information Management, 52*,.

Stulz, R. M. (2019). FinTech, bigtech, and the future of banks. *Journal of Applied Corporate Finance, 31*(4), 86–97.

Thomson Reuters. (2016). *Know your customer surveys reveal escalating costs and complexity*. Available at: https://www.thomsonreuters.com/en/press-releases/2016/may/thomson-reuters-2016-know-your-customer-surveys.html.

Vermeulen, P. (2004). Managing product innovation in financial services firms. *European Management Journal, 22*(1), 43–50.

Yeoh, P. (2017). Regulatory issues in blockchain technology. *Journal of Financial Regulation and Compliance, 25*(2), 196–208.

Yermack, D. (2019). *Blockchain technology's potential in the financial system*. Prepared for the Federal Reserve Bank of Atlanta, 2019 Financial Market's Conference, Amelia Island, FL. May 20, 2019. Available at: https://www.frbatlanta.org/news/conferences-and-events/conferences/2019/0519-financial-markets-conference/-/media/1B59605EE1E946C6909F505A8341EB04.ashx.

CHAPTER 4

Blockchain and Banking Business Models

Abstract This chapter explores the potential impact that blockchain's DLT can have on traditional banking business models. Building on the Business Model Canvas framework developed by Osterwalder and Pigneur (Business model generation: A handbook for visionaries, game changers, and challengers. John Wiley & Sons, 2010), this chapter outlines how blockchain technology can affect all elements of a bank's business model and lead to new business models in banking. Moreover, the chapter provides an overview of the current status of banks' adoption of the technology and highlights their approach to handling the challenges of blockchain.

Keywords Blockchain · Distributed ledger technology · Banking business models · Business model innovation · Canvas

4.1 Introduction

The emergence of new innovation technologies has changed traditional banking business models: these new technologies have significantly altered traditional processes across the value chain—from the way banks interact with customers to how they organise their middle and bank-office operations (Kobler et al. 2016).

P. Martino, *Blockchain and Banking*,
https://doi.org/10.1007/978-3-030-70970-9_4

As a new innovation technology, blockchain has been acknowledged as a disruptive force for the financial sector because it could potentially reshape existing business models in the financial services industry—in banks, in particular. This chapter outlines how blockchain's distributed ledger technology could reshape traditional banking business models. The framework developed by Osterwalder and Pigneur (2010), which they call the Business Model Canvas, is used for this purpose. The chapter concludes with an overview of the status of banks' adoption of blockchain and discusses the practices they have undertaken to embrace the technology.

4.2 Technological Development and Business Model Innovation

A company's business model, generally understood as the way a firm creates, delivers and captures value (Osterwalder and Pigneur 2010; Zott and Amit 2010; Teece 2018), changes and adapts over time in line with the market conditions. Among several factors, technological progress has been largely acknowledged as one of the main sources of change in organisations' business models (Calia et al. 2007; Teece 2010; Nowiński and Kozma 2017).

The emergence of new innovation technologies can allow the development of new ways to create and deliver value, including changes in how a firm organises and engages in economic exchanges, as well as the ways in which firms interact with their suppliers and customers (Amit and Zott, 2001; Calia et al. 2007; Zott et al. 2011). Literature refers to this as business model innovation (e.g. Lindgardt et al. 2009; Amit and Zott 2012; Loebbecke and Picot 2015; Foss and Saebi 2017): the result of an innovation initiative that revises an organisation's existing business model (e.g. initiatives to optimise existing processes to increase the overall efficiency and quality of products and services) or completely changes it (e.g. by serving new market segments and developing new products and services). Thus, business model innovation implies a new configuration of what is done in the company and how it is done to offer customers a new value proposition.

The digital revolution in the banking industry, whose customers are increasingly adapting to new technologies and new types of competitors and solutions arising in the space, undermines the traditional schemes used by intermediaries offering financial services (Kobler et al. 2016;

EBA 2018; Bank of Italy 2020). On the one hand, significant changes in consumer expectations and behaviours are pushing to reconfigure the bank–customer relationship model. Immediacy, simplicity and accessibility needs guide the choices for purchasing and using banking services and focus the attention of banks' customers on a better-quality and more customised offer. On the other hand, new technologies are allowing many new players to enter the market, including non-financial service providers and fintech start-ups, which are offering financial services with much lower costs and a better user experience than traditional intermediaries. As a result, competition is increasing, which makes it ever more important for banks to satisfy new customer needs.

Thus, the banking industry is in the midst of significant changes that require banks to substantially rethink their business models and strategies in order to cope with these developments. The rise in blockchain's distributed ledger technology (DLT) has also played an important role. As a new innovation technology, blockchain has been widely acknowledged as a key source of future financial system innovation (McKinsey 2016; Iansiti and Lakhani 2017; Philippon 2016; Lewis et al. 2017) with the potential to transform existing business models across many industries (Holotiuk et al. 2017; Nowiński and Kozma 2017; Morkunas et al. 2019)—the banking industry, in particular (Rajnak and Puschmann 2020). Blockchain can revolutionise how banks create and deliver products and services and, thus, offer opportunities for new value creation.

The following paragraph discusses how blockchain's DLT can lead to business model innovation in banks.

4.3 Blockchain and Innovation in the Banking Business Models

In line with Morkunas et al. (2019), the Business Model Canvas (BMC) developed by Osterwalder and Pigneur (2010) is used here to explore blockchain's potential implications for traditional banking business models. The BMC, defined as a description of "the rationale of how an organization creates, delivers, and captures value" (Osterwalder and Pigneur 2010, p. 14), represents the elements of a company's business model, as well as their potential interconnections and impact on value creation. It consists of nine interconnected building blocks covering the four main areas of a business: offer, customers, infrastructure and financial viability (Osterwalder and Pigneur 2002). These building blocks, as

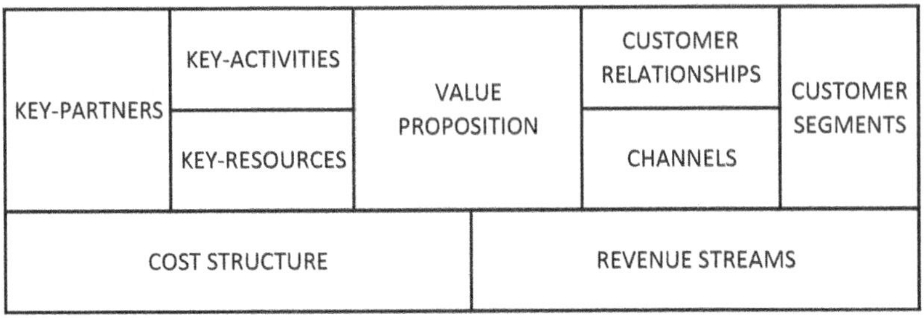

Fig. 4.1 The business model canvas (Osterwalder and Pigneur 2010)

shown in Fig. 4.1, are: (1) value proposition, (2) customer segments, (3) channels, (4) customer relationships, (5) key resources, (6) key activities, (7) key partnerships, (8) revenue streams and (9) cost structure.

This framework has been widely adopted by both practitioners and researchers (e.g. Abraham 2013; Massa and Tucci 2013; Sort and Nielsen 2018; Keane et al. 2018; Morkunas et al. 2019) in several contexts, and it is widely recommended by academic incubators and venture capital associations worldwide (Cosenz 2017). Thanks to its readability and because the framework makes it easy to describe an organisation's business model, it is an effective tool to communicate a business's strategy and organisation (Cosenz 2017). Moreover, it facilitates the exploration of potential innovations to the business model itself (Joyce and Paquin 2016). For instance, building on this framework, a recent study by Morkunas et al. (2019) explores the influence that blockchain can have on a firm's business model; the study lays out which opportunities the technology offers for a firm's value creation by having an impact on every facet of the business model.

Thus, the BMC can be an effective tool to understand how blockchain might affect a bank's business model. The following subsections contain a discussion of how each of the BMC's nine essential elements could be affected by blockchain's DLT.

1. Value proposition

   The *value proposition* building block describes "the bundle of products and services that create value for a specific customer segment". A firm value proposition, which can be innovative or similar to existing market offers but with added features and attributes, is one reason why customers turn to one business instead of another.

As mentioned in Chapter 3, blockchain allows banks to enhance the products and services that they can offer their customers. By automating parts of bank's business processes (e.g. through smart contracts) and eliminating the intermediaries involved in transactions, blockchain enables banks to provide their services and products in a faster, low-cost and secure way, thereby improving customers' experience. The trade finance transaction made in 2018 between HSBC and ING Bank supports this argument: the two banks completed the world's first commercially viable trade finance transaction in a record time of 24 hours instead of the standard period of 5–10 days, thereby providing benefits for the companies involved in the transaction in terms of speed and ease of execution.

However, blockchain can also allow banks to offer a new value proposition to their customers. In particular, it can bring innovation to the banking sector by allowing banks to create products and services that were previously unavailable. Having access to a range of information recorded in the ledger (i.e. information not only of their customers but also of other organisations such as ships, ports and insurance), banks can exploit this information to have a better and more complete understanding of the behaviours, needs and preferences of their customers. This, in turn, enables banks to create and offer new products and services that are not necessarily associated with traditional banking products but tailored to meet the customers' individual needs.

Thus, in addition to improving existing banking services and products, blockchain can help banks to offer a new value proposition to their customers by creating high-value-added products and services that can provide a big competitive edge.

2. Customer segments

Osterwalder and Pigneur (2010) define the *customer segments* building block as "the different groups of people or organizations that an enterprise aims to reach and serve". They represent the target audiences that a company plans to offer value to their products and services.

It has been highlighted that blockchain's DLT can enable banks to serve their existing customer bases more efficiently. By reducing times and costs in transactions, blockchain technology enhances the products and services that banks can offer to their customers, particularly in areas such as lending, payments, trade finance and capital markets.

For banks, however, one of the key advantages of blockchain technology is the opportunity to open new market segments, which allows them to reach a multitude of new potential customers. This potential target market accounts for about 2 billion financially excluded individuals worldwide (i.e. unbanked and underbanked populations), for whom blockchain can make banking more accessible. Through blockchain, banks can reach these excluded populations by solving most of the challenges they face when trying to access financial services (e.g. problems linked to KYC processes) and providing banking product and services tailored to their needs (e.g. by offering new financial alternatives, like cryptocurrencies, at an affordable price). Studies (Accenture 2015; EY 2017) estimate that banks could generate \$200 billion to \$380 billion in new annual revenues by bringing today's excluded individuals and businesses into the formal banking sector.

Hence, blockchain can offer banks the opportunity to reach a multitude of potential customers, thereby generating new revenues streams.

3. Channels

The *channels* building block "describes how a company communicates with and reaches its customer segments to deliver a value proposition". It consists of a company's interface with its customers, including communication, distribution and sales channels.

Recent advances in communication and information technology have considerably altered the way that banks interact with their customers. New technologies have contributed to the introduction of new digital services available both online and on apps to increase customer acquisition and facilitate access to services. This has also led to an optimisation of (i.e. reduction in) banks' branch physical network. In this regard, blockchain technology can further contribute to this change instead of revising or completely transforming banks' interface with their customers. This means that blockchain will boost the digitalisation process of banks' communication and distribution channels, shifting them to online platforms and thereby allowing banks to reduce the number of physical branches.

4. Customer relationships

   The *customer relationships* building block "describes the types of relationships that a company establishes with specific customer segments" (Osterwalder and Pigneur 2010). These relationships may be driven by a motivation to acquire customers, retain them or boost sales.

   To enhance their ability to acquire and exploit knowledge about their customers, which is essential to forging personalised relationships, banks have directed their efforts towards improving their customer relationship management (CRM) practices. To this end, many banks have heavily invested in new technologies to improve efficiency in CRM practices and automate their database management, front office operations, marketing activities, etc.

   Blockchain's DLT can contribute in this regard. Thanks to its key characteristics, blockchain can allow banks to store customer data (e.g. contact information, products used and interactions) more securely than traditional methods and, thus, improve personal data security. This improved trust between banks and customers is essential to increase customers' willingness to share their personal data with banks. Moreover, blockchain can help to update customer profiles in real time when new information is recorded in the ledger and make information distributed and accessible to everyone within the organisation. This can allow banks to monitor and serve their clients more proactively and implement customer-centric strategies: with blockchain, each department can access the same information (data on deposits, loans, etc.) across all customer profiles, which provides a single view of every customer account, thereby providing deeper insights into their habits and personal preferences. In turn, banks are better able to align their product and sales strategies with their customers' requirements and preferences.
5. Key resources

   Osterwalder and Pigneur (2010) define *key resources* as "the most important assets required to make a business model work". According to them, key resources allow a company to create and offer a value proposition, reach markets, maintain relationships with customer segments and earn revenues.

   The adoption of blockchain technology will require banks to reconsider the key resources that make up their business model. Since different (physical, financial, intellectual or human) key resources are needed depending on the type of business model (Osterwalder and Pigneur 2010), banks will need to move outside their traditional resources in order to improve their capabilities to deal with a radical innovation like blockchain, which can change the way banks do business. In this regard, ***human resources*** capable of interpreting blockchain challenges and translating them into benefits for banks will be key enablers for a new business model.

Although blockchain may jeopardise some traditional banking jobs (e.g. those involving tasks like processing and reconciling transactions and verifying documentation) and cause others to change (e.g. auditors), it will also require new resources never had before (Bank of Italy 2020). In particular, banks will need resources—blockchain experts, technologists and IT experts, among others—who understand the technology and can translate it into costs and economy of scale. Most importantly, they will also need resources (e.g. data scientists) to elaborate and exploit the vast and diversified quantity of information recorded in the distributed ledger to create new products and solutions for the banks' customers.

To this end, many banks are already requiring new professional profiles with these skills and expertise and are establishing new figures within the top management team in these areas (e.g. Chief Transformation Officer, Chief Data Officer etc.). Nevertheless, it is worth noting that these resources, including blockchain experts, are still scarce and difficult to acquire given the increased competition with fintech start-ups and other financial companies. Therefore, they can represent a key source of competitive edge for banks.

6. Key activities

The ***key activities*** building block is defined as "the most important things a company must do to make its business model work". They are the most important activities that allow companies to operate successfully. According to Osterwalder and Pigneur (2010), key activities and key resources are crucial to creating and offering a value proposition and reaching markets.

As highlighted before, blockchain can allow banks to generate a new value proposition for their customers. This ability is particularly dependent on the vast variety of information recorded in the ledger—information pertaining not only to their clients but also to the other organisations. Given that the information is crucial to better understanding their customers' needs, exploiting these data can help banks to provide new products and personalised services with higher value added. Accordingly, activities like *data analytics* and *research & development* will be key enablers of the new value proposition. Banks will have to invest more in such activities, which are crucial for developing new products—not necessarily associated with traditional banking products (e.g. insurance products)—and innovative solutions to satisfy new customer needs.

In this regard, it will also be essential to create a trust circle with customers, which would give access to even more customer data. Hence, the role of *CRM* in banks also needs to change: CRM can no longer be a separate tool used to track commercial activities and customer information but will be a key activity to deliver value to customers by helping banks manage customers and better understand their needs to provide the right solutions. This will improve how banks segment, target, acquire and retain their customers.

Finally, it was observed that access to IT expertise, technology talents and data scientists is becoming a key challenge for banks as the current growth in technology-based projects creates an ever greater demand for technology talent at a pace that outweighs the supply. Banks need to find ways to attract and retain such key personnel. Activities involving human resources, such as *recruitment* and *training*, will also be crucial for banks in this new context to facilitate the implementation of innovative business models. Banks will have to focus on skills and expertise (e.g. blockchain experts, data analytics, etc.) that are different from those of traditional banking (e.g. banking and finance, risk management, etc.) and, more importantly, difficult to attract given the increasing competition. It will be also necessary to translate the skills of such professional figures in the financial field. Moreover, the existing workforce in banks needs to adapt to this new context. Knowledge about blockchain will have to be disseminated within the organisation while a strong "data and digital-focused culture" is developed and built to foster the development of innovative solutions.

7. Key partnerships

The *key partnerships* building block describes "the network of suppliers and partners that make the business model work". These partnerships, created to optimise companies' business models, reduce risk and acquire resources, can take different forms, including strategic alliances, strategic partnerships between competitors and buyer–supplier relationships to ensure reliable supplies.

The adoption of blockchain technology can change or add new types of key partnerships for banks. Above all, collaboration with fintech start-ups—especially blockchain-based platforms—is crucial for banks to acquire particular resources or perform certain activities. As an example, it is worth mentioning the partnership between the UK-based Lloyds Bank and Komgo, a blockchain-based platform that digitises and streamlines international trade and commodity finance. Komgo enables businesses to quickly and automatically exchange data and associated documents across a wide range of solutions (from letters of credit and KYC management to receivables discounting) in a digital, secure and decentralised way. The partnership makes it possible for the bank to use blockchain for quicker international commodity trade finance. Collaborations with fintech also allow banks to utilise emerging technologies (e.g. blockchain applications) and continuously incubate new ideas to meet the changing needs of their customers.

Moreover, blockchain can open the doors for strategic partnerships between competitors (not only with other banks but also with other actors in the financial chain, like insurance companies), which is necessary to allow for the technology to be widely adopted and to further develop its applications.

Finally, partnerships with universities and research centres can be key for a bank to get a competitive edge (Martino 2019). While banks can provide support for academic research and technical development, as well as innovation in blockchain and its main applications, universities can provide key resources (human capital) for banks by developing the necessary knowledge and expertise (especially IT skills) to deal with the challenges of blockchain. An example in this area is the cooperation between Bank Frick, a bank in Liechtenstein, and the University of Liechtenstein through the "Blockchain and FinTech certificate programme" created for the application-oriented transfer of knowledge to help with the technological redesign of existing financial systems. Initiatives like this can play an important role in imparting the latest knowledge and skills to deal with new technologies such as blockchain and its applications (e.g. smart contracts).

8. Revenue streams

   The building block *revenue streams* describes "the ways a company generates cash from each customer segment".

   Blockchain technology has the potential to change how a bank generates revenue. First, as mentioned above, blockchain can enable a bank to open new market segments (i.e. unbanked and underbanked populations) and, consequently, reach many potential customers and generate additional streams of revenue. Moreover, banks can increase their revenues by extending their traditional banking services and product volumes. In particular, by improving banking processes' efficiency and, consequently, reducing the operational costs involved in transactions, banks can reduce the commissions they charge their customers since the costs will be lower. This allows banks using blockchain technology to provide their services (e.g. cross-border payments) at a lower cost than their competitors and secure a major competitive advantage.

   Second, blockchain can generate new revenue streams for banks by bringing innovation to the sector: by exploiting the information recorded in the distributed ledger, banks can create new products and solutions for their customers that do not exist yet, thereby adding value to their customers' experience. This is the real benefit of blockchain for banks (Martino 2019). Product innovation can become key elements of banks' strategy and a new source of competitive edge.

9. Cost structure

   The final building block is the firm's *cost structure*, which "describes all costs incurred to operate a business model".

   Cost structure is the most important business model element that can be affected by the adoption of blockchain's DLT. It enables substantial cost savings for banks by improving banking processes' efficiency (Morkunas et al. 2019; Martino 2019; Rajnak and Puschmann 2020). By automating parts of inter-organisational processes and eliminating the intermediaries involved in transactions, blockchain can help to significantly reduce bank infrastructure and the operating costs associated with several banking areas. By improving efficiencies in several banking areas and operations, such as international money transfers, trade finance, syndicated lending, securities trading and regulatory compliance, savings could total between \$15 billion and \$20 billion a year by 2022, according to research by Santander InnoVentures, Oliver Wyman and the Anthemis Group (2015).

Thus, blockchain's DLT has the potential to revolutionise banks' cost infrastructure with significant benefits for their profitability.

4.4 Banks' Approach to Blockchain's Challenges

The discussion in the previous paragraph suggests that the potential impact of blockchain's DLT on the traditional banking business model could be significant, with all elements of the Business Model Canvas significantly affected. Blockchain can allow banks to offer a new value proposition to their customers, extend their customer bases and improve the efficiency of internal processes, thereby generating significant benefits for the banks' profitability.

Banks have acknowledged the potential benefits of blockchain's DLT and are looking for opportunities in this area.

Today, blockchain is on the agenda of many large banks that are investing in and experimenting with this technology. Investments include *studies* on blockchain to explore how to implement and leverage the technology, *proofs of concept* through which banks are experimenting with uses of the technology (albeit on a very small scale and in a controlled environment) and *pilots* in which the technology is used for real transactions, typically with a limited duration and number of participants (Mills et al. 2016; Martino 2019). The banks have taken different approaches (Mills et al. 2016; EBA 2018): many have organised dedicated teams internally to study and experiment with the technology and/or established innovation labs to understand its potential costs and benefits, while others are collaborating with or investing directly in fintech start-ups to access the technology. At the same time, several banks are also participating in blockchain consortia/alliances (e.g. R3 and Enterprise Ethereum Alliance) in which several banks, as well as other stakeholders, work together to explore the potential benefits of blockchain and test solutions—in cooperation instead of in silos—to mutualise the costs and risks associated with the development of blockchain arrangements.

Blockchain is developing at a rapid pace in the banking industry; in most cases, however, the technology is still in the development phase (J.P. Morgan 2018). For instance, in the EU context, the European Banking Authority's (2019) risk assessment report on the European

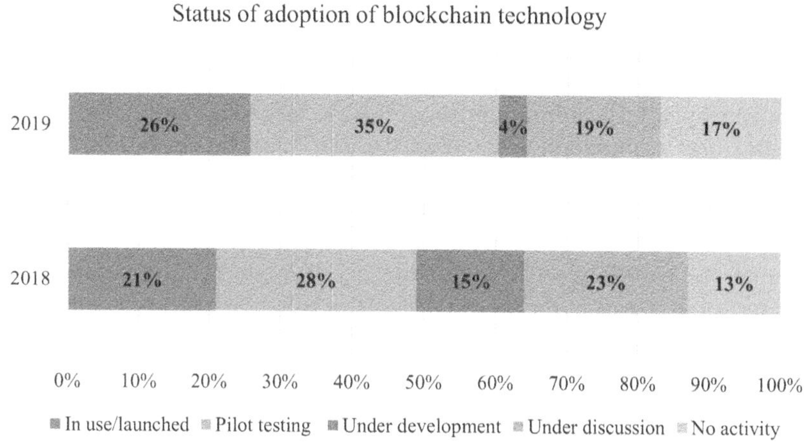

Fig. 4.2 Status of adoption of blockchain's distributed ledger technology by EU banks (*Source* Own processing of data from the EBA's [2019] risk assessment report of the European banking system)

banking system shows that, in 2019, only 26% of the sample[1] analysed was using blockchain's distributed ledger, while the majority of banks (39%) were in the "pilot testing" or "in development" stages, as shown in Fig. 4.2.

At present, it is still difficult to assess how and to what extent blockchain's DLT affects traditional banking business models. Recent evidence (EBA 2018; Bank of Italy 2019; Rajnak and Puschmann 2020) suggests that banks' investments in new technologies, including blockchain's DLT, have different objectives. In some cases, investments aim to improve existing business models by making processes and functions more efficient: by employing new technologies, the banks are working to digitalise and optimise operations, reduce their own operating costs and enhance efficiency gains. In other cases, the aim of investing is to entirely reshape business models or develop new ones. The ultimate goal of these projects is to satisfy changing customer demands and find new streams of revenue. This implies developing a new value proposition,

[1] Data derive from the Risk Assessment Questionnaire (RAQ) conducted by the EBA on a semi-annual basis. Answers to the questionnaires were provided by 65 European banks and 13 market analysts in September and October 2019.

serving new market segments and developing new ways to interact with customers in order to enhance the customer experience.

Moreover, limitations on the widespread adoption of blockchain remain in place, including regulatory issues, technical hurdles (e.g. scalability) and technological standardisation. Thus, the extent to which blockchain can affect traditional banking business models will also depend on how such challenges will be addressed. In this regard, as I will discuss in Chapter 5, it is worth pointing out that regulators and authorities around the world are actively working to promote the development of the technology within the existing regulatory framework, while banks are collaborating with each other and with other stakeholders (governments, regulators, universities, etc.) to develop common base standards that will allow interoperability across the different DLT arrangements necessary to facilitate the broad adoption of blockchain by banks.

4.5 Conclusions

Building on the Business Model Canvas framework by Osterwalder and Pigneur (2010), this chapter provided a discussion of the potential impact of blockchain's distributed ledger technology on the traditional banking business model.

Because business model innovation occurs once some of a company's business model elements have been changed and a novel logic of how a company creates, delivers and captures value has been launched (Lindgardt et al. 2009; Amit and Zott 2012; Loebbecke and Picot 2015; Foss and Saebi 2017), the results of the analysis suggest that blockchain's potential impact on banks' business model could be broad; all the elements of the business models (i.e. how banks generate profits, which customers they serve and which distribution channels they use) can be significantly affected. The DLT of blockchain could allow banks to change how financial services are offered and, thus, improve their traditional competitive advantages. In particular, blockchain can help banks to offer a new value proposition to their customers, providing traditional products and services more efficiently and creating new ones, as well as extend their customer bases with significant benefits in terms of the banks' profitability. In turn, this will compel banks to focus on new resources and activities and establish new partnerships to enable a new value proposition.

In line with previous studies (e.g. Morkunas et al. 2019; Rajnak and Puschmann 2020), this study suggests that blockchain may lead to new business models in banking and a challenge to the status quo. Nevertheless, it is still difficult to assess how and to what extent blockchain can affect the traditional banking business model. Although the use of blockchain continues to spread, with numerous large banks investing in the technology, recent evidence shows that blockchain projects in banks are still in the development phase. Thus, the technology does not yet represent a key element in the banks' strategy and is, for the time being, not affecting their business models. The next two to three years will be key to understanding its real impact on the banking industry.

References

Abraham, S. (2013). Will business model innovation replace strategic analysis? *Strategy & Leadership, 41*(2), 31–38. Available at: https://doi.org/10.1108/10878571311318222.

Accenture. (2015). *Billion reasons to bank inclusively*. Available at: https://www.accenture.com/us-en/_acnmedia/Accenture/Conversion-Assets/DotCom/Documents/Global/PDF/Dualpub_22/Accenture-billion-reasons-bank-inclusively.pdf.

Amit, R., & Zott, C. (2001). Value creation in e-business. *Strategic Management Journal, 22*(6–7), 493–520.

Amit, R., & Zott, C. (2012). *Creating value through business model innovation*. Available at: http://marketing.mitsmr.com/PDF/STR0715-Top-10-Strategy.pdf#page=38.

Bank of Italy. (2019). *Indagine fintech nel sistema finanziario italiano*. Available at: https://www.bancaditalia.it/compiti/vigilanza/analisi-sistema/approfondimenti-banche-int/Allegato_2_Indagine_Fintech.pdf.

Bank of Italy. (2020). *FinTech, rischi e opportunità per i giovani futuri manager bancari*. Intervento di Alessandra Perrazzelli, Vice Direttrice Generale della Banca d'Italia. Lectio Magistralis, Università di Genova, 24 gennaio 2020. Available at: https://www.bancaditalia.it/pubblicazioni/interventi-direttorio/int-dir-2020/Perrazzelli-24.01.2020.pdf.

Calia, R. C., Guerrini, F. M., & Moura, G. L. (2007). Innovation networks: From technological development to business model reconfiguration. *Technovation, 27*(8), 426–432.

Cosenz, F. (2017). Supporting start-up business model design through system dynamics modelling. *Management Decision, 55*(1), 57–80. https://doi.org/10.1108/MD-06-2016-0395.

EBA. (2018). *Report on the impact of fintech on incumbent credit institutions' business models*. Available at: https://eba.europa.eu/sites/default/documents/files/documents/10180/2270909/1f27bb57-387e-4978-82f6-ece725 b51941/Report%20on%20the%20impact%20of%20Fintech%20on%20incumbent%20credit%20institutions%27%20business%20models.pdf?retry=1.

EBA. (2019). *Risk assessment of the European banking system*, November 2019. Available at: https://eba.europa.eu/sites/default/documents/files/document_library/Risk%20Analysis%20and%20Data/EU%20Wide%20Transparency%20Exercise/2019/Transparency%20exercise%20documents/Risk_Assessment_Report_November_2019.PDF.

EY. (2017). *Innovation in financial inclusion revenue growth through innovative inclusion*.

Foss, N. J., & Saebi, T. (2017). Fifteen years of research on business model innovation: How far have we come, and where should we go? *Journal of Management, 43*(1), 200–227.

Holotiuk, F., Pisani, F., & Moormann, J. (2017). *The impact of blockchain technology on business models in the payments industry*. In Proceedings of 13th International Conference on Wirtschaftsinformatik, St. Gallen, 12–15 February, pp. 912–926.

Iansiti, M., & Lakhani, K. R. (2017). The truth about blockchain. *Harvard Business Review, 95*(1), 118–127.

J.P. Morgan's Corporate Finance Advisory, Digital Investment Banking, and Blockchain Center of Excellence teams. (2018). *Blockchain and the decentralization revolution A CFO's guide to the potential implications of distributed ledger technology*. Available at: https://www.jpmorgan.com/solutions/cib/investment-banking/corporate-finance-advisory/blockchain.

Joyce, A., & Paquin, R. L. (2016). The triple layered business model canvas: A tool to design more sustainable business models. *Journal of Cleaner Production, 135*, 1474–1486.

Keane, S. F., Cormican, K. T., & Sheahan, J. N. (2018). Comparing how entrepreneurs and managers represent the elements of the business model canvas. *Journal of Business Venturing Insights, 9*, 65–74.

Kobler, D., Bucherer, S., Scholtmann, J. (2016). *Banking business models of the future*. Available at: https://www2.deloitte.com/content/dam/Deloitte/tw/Documents/financial-services/tw-bankingbusiness-models-of-the-future-2016.pdf.

Lewis, R., McPartland, J. and Ranjan, R. (2017). Blockchain and financial market innovation. *Economic Perspectives, 41*(7), 1–17. Federal Reserve Bank of Chicago.

Lindgardt, Z., Reeves, M., Stalk, G., & Deimler, M. S. (2009). *Business model innovation. When the game gets tough, change the game*. Boston, MA: The Boston Consulting Group.

Loebbecke, C., & Picot, A. (2015). Reflections on societal and business model transformation arising from digitization and big data analytics: A research agenda. *The Journal of Strategic Information Systems, 24*(3), 149–157.

Martino, P. (2019). Blockchain technology: Challenges and opportunities for banks. *International Journal of Financial Innovation in Banking, 2*(4), 314–333.

Massa, L., & Tucci, C. L. (2013). Business model innovation. *The Oxford Handbook of Innovation Management, 20*(18), 420–441.

McKinsey & Company. (2016). *How blockchains could change the world*. Available at: https://www.mckinsey.com/industries/high-tech/our-insights/how-blockchains-could-changethe-world.

Mills, D., Wang, K., Malone, B., et al. (2016). *Distributed ledger technology in payments, clearing, and settlement*. Finance and Economics Discussion Series 2016–095. Washington: Board of Governors of the Federal Reserve System, https://doi.org/10.17016/FEDS.2016.095.

Morkunas, V. J., Paschen, J., & Boon, E. (2019). How blockchain technologies impact your business model. *Business Horizons, 62*(3), 295–306.

Nowiński, W., & Kozma, M. (2017). How can blockchain technology disrupt the existing business models? *Entrepreneurial Business and Economics Review, 5*(3), 173–188.

Osterwalder, A., & Pigneur, Y. (2002). *An eBusiness model ontology for modeling eBusiness*. BLED 2002 proceedings, 2.

Osterwalder, A., & Pigneur, Y. (2010). *Business model generation: A handbook for visionaries, game changers, and challengers*. John Wiley & Sons.

Philippon, T. (2016). *The fintech opportunity*, National Bureau of Economic Research Working Paper No. 22476. Available at: http://www.nber.org/papers/w22476.pdf.

Rajnak, V., & Puschmann, T. (2020). The impact of blockchain on business models in banking. *Information Systems and e-Business Management*, 1–53.

Santander InnoVentures, Oliver Wyman and Anthemis Group. (2015). *The fintech 2.0 paper: Rebooting financial services*. Available at: https://www.finextra.com/finextra-downloads/newsdocs/the%20fintech%202%200%20paper.pdf.

Sort, J. C., & Nielsen, C. (2018). Using the business model canvas to improve investment processes. *Journal of Research in Marketing and Entrepreneurship, 20*(1).

Teece, D. J. (2010). Business models, business strategy and innovation. *Long Range Planning, 43*(2–3), 172–194.

Teece, D. J. (2018). Business models and dynamic capabilities. *Long Range Planning, 51*(1), 40–49.

Zott, C., & Amit, R. (2010). Business model design: An activity system perspective. *Long Range Planning, 43*(2–3), 216–226.

Zott, C., Amit, R., & Massa, L. (2011). The business model: Recent developments and future research. *Journal of Management, 37*(4), 1019–1042.

CHAPTER 5

Regulation of Blockchain Technology: An Overview

Abstract The adoption of blockchain technology by the banking industry entails significant regulatory issues, since the technology can pose several challenges to existing legal and regulatory frameworks. This chapter addresses the main regulatory issues in blockchain technology. After presenting the main risks and problems associated with the use of the technology and its main applications, the chapter outlines the responses undertaken by regulators and authorities around the world with a specific focus on both the US and the EU context.

Keywords Blockchain · Distributed ledger technology · Cryptocurrencies · Smart contracts · Regulation

5.1 Introduction

Blockchain technology and its primary forms of application (i.e. cryptocurrencies and smart contracts) are changing many facets of finance, including retail and wholesale payments, financial market infrastructures, credit provision and capital raising, among others (FSB 2019b). Chapter 3 highlighted that blockchain can benefit banks in several ways: efficiency improvement, product innovation and the ability to reach new customers. It can also pose new risks related to the increasing competition between

P. Martino, *Blockchain and Banking*,
https://doi.org/10.1007/978-3-030-70970-9_5

blockchain-based companies that provide banking services. Nevertheless, it has been noted that the opportunities and risks presented by blockchain are tied to significant regulatory issues since its adoption can challenge the existing legal and regulatory framework, and such challenges must be addressed before blockchain is adopted. This is particularly true for highly regulated sectors like banking, which is characterised by forms of centralised control where central authorities (e.g. central banks) are accountable and responsible for providing the services to all the other participants.

This chapter describes the main regulatory challenges of blockchain technology and provides an overview of how regulators and authorities around the world are tackling them, although the specific focus will be on the US and European Union (EU) context. Regulatory issues deriving from first-generation blockchain—i.e. blockchain used to launch cryptocurrencies (in general, public blockchains)—are different from those deriving from second-generation blockchain—i.e. the adoption of blockchain's distributed ledger technology (DLT) to provide banking services (in general, private blockchains). Therefore, their regulatory implications and related responses will be discussed separately.

5.2 Regulatory Issues and Cryptocurrencies

One of the main concerns that regulators and policymakers have about blockchain technology has to do with cryptocurrencies, which can allow users to avoid regulation and engage in misconduct. As highlighted in Chapter 3, owing to its anonymity, cross-border nature and quick transferability, the use of blockchain in cryptocurrencies is well suited to illicit activities such as fraud and manipulation, tax evasion, hacking, money laundering and funding for terrorist activities[1] (Houben and Snyers 2018).

Above all, the anonymity inherent in public blockchains, which varies from complete anonymity to pseudo-anonymity, can prevent cryptocurrency transactions from being adequately monitored, thus allowing transactions to occur outside the regulatory perimeter and, consequently, enabling individuals to use cryptocurrencies for unlawful activities. As reported in the European Commission's Impact Assessment (EC 2016)

[1] Such risks are tied not to the blockchain itself, however, but rather to the nature of cryptocurrencies.

accompanying its Anti-Money Laundering Directive (AMLD5) proposal, the anonymity surrounding virtual currencies imposes an intrinsic limitation on identification and monitoring possibilities, given that authorities are unable to link identities with transactions, which generates a problem regarding transaction traceability. Meanwhile, for issues related to anti-terrorism and tax avoidance, among others, banks must adhere to strict regulations associated with Know Your Customer (KYC) and anti-money laundering (AML) laws: they must track transactions step by step and should be able to identify the actors involved in transactions to safeguard financial systems and customers and increase transparency. In addition, the intrinsically cross-border nature of blockchain represents another major challenge for regulators since decentralisation could boost the degree to which financial services are provided across borders, thereby intensifying jurisdictional uncertainty. Cryptocurrency transactions can also be carried out in jurisdictions that do not have effective controls against money laundering and terrorist financing, which raises questions about regulatory enforcement of misconduct. As a result, regulators around the world are trying to define cryptocurrencies' scope to avoid their use for illicit activities.

5.3 Regulation of Cryptocurrencies

Today, regulators around the world are responding to the emerging risks associated with the use of blockchain technology to launch cryptocurrencies. They aim to prevent theft, fraud, market manipulation and money laundering (PWC 2018; French and Stettner 2019). To date, there has not been a common taxonomy of cryptocurrencies or a shared understanding of how they should be treated from a regulatory standpoint (ECB 2019). The legal status of cryptocurrencies varies by country, and the variety of approaches ranges from total bans to regulating support for the particular activity. The following subsections present an overview of the different approaches that regulators have undertaken in various countries.

5.3.1 US Regulatory Approach to Cryptocurrencies

In the US context, the regulation of cryptocurrencies has evolved into a multi-faceted and multi-regulatory approach, since its scope falls under different authorities (Beauchamp et al. 2019) depending on whether cryptocurrencies are considered as securities, commodities or currencies. In December 2019, to clarify which federal agencies regulate cryptocurrencies and, consequently, establish their areas of regulatory oversight, the "Crypto-Currency Act of 2020" was introduced to define categories of crypto-assets and specify the federal regulatory agencies authorised to regulate them. The discussion draft of this bill introduced new definitions for categories of crypto-assets like "crypto-commodity", "crypto-currency" and "crypto-security" and assigned each category to a sole regulator: the Commodity Futures Trading Commission (CFTC) would have the authority to regulate crypto-commodities; the Secretary of the Treasury, acting through the US Department of the Treasury's Financial Crimes Enforcement Network (FinCEN), would have the authority to regulate cryptocurrencies; and the Securities and Exchange Commission (SEC) would be able to regulate crypto-securities.

These authorities have actively addressed regulatory issues associated with cryptocurrency activities by taking several measures and issuing numerous enforcement actions to bring transparency and integrity to the cryptocurrency markets and deter and prosecute fraud and abuse.

First, the SEC has been monitoring cryptocurrencies, particularly with regard to initial coin offerings (ICOs), to prevent fraud and other misconduct. Depending on the nature of the digital asset, including the rights it purports to convey and how it is offered and sold, the SEC provides that cryptocurrencies may be defined as a security under the US federal securities laws and, thus, would fall under SEC's jurisdiction of enforcing federal securities laws. Accordingly, like any other activity involving an offering of securities, ICOs that represent offerings of securities must comply with the registration requirements of the Securities Act; they must be accompanied by the important disclosures, processes and other investor protections that US securities laws require (SEC 2017). This implies that such offerings and sales have to either be registered with the SEC[2] or qualify for an exemption from registration. However, even if no registration is required, activities involving digital assets that are securities may still be subject to the commission's regulation and oversight. Furthermore, the SEC provides that a platform permitting trade in digital assets that are securities and operating as an "exchange", as defined by the federal securities laws, must register with the SEC as a national

[2] The registration provisions require that people disclose certain information to investors and that the information be complete and not materially misleading.

securities exchange. It is subject to cybersecurity requirements and obligations to have policies around preventing fraudulent and manipulative acts and practices unless it is exempt from registration (SEC 2018; PWC 2018). In 2019, the SEC's Strategic Hub for Innovation and Financial Technology (FinHub) published guidance providing a framework to help market participants assess whether a digital asset is offered and sold as an "investment contract"[3] and, therefore, whether their offers and sales can be considered securities transactions (SEC 2019).

Second, the CFTC has exercised its authority over cryptocurrencies concerning derivatives markets. In 2014, the CFTC declared cryptocurrencies to be a "commodity" subject to oversight under its authority under the Commodity Exchange Act (CFTC 2018), thus extending the CFTC's jurisdiction and regulatory framework over market participants' proper registration, as well as fraudulent and manipulation activities, to the digital assets industry. This means that the CFTC has jurisdiction when a virtual currency is used in a derivatives contract or if there is fraud or manipulation involving a virtual currency traded in interstate commerce. Taking a similar approach to the SEC, the CFTC has mainly issued enforcement actions to prevent fraud and other abuse such as the misappropriation of funds in derivative markets and has issued numerous enforcement cases (PWC 2018; Lucking and Aravind 2020). For instance, the CFTC has taken action against unregistered cryptocurrency exchanges (e.g. BitFinex) and enforced the laws prohibiting wash trading and prearranged trades on a derivatives platform. It has also issued proposed guidance on what a derivative market is and what qualifies as a spot market in the virtual currency context, as well as warnings about valuations and volatility in spot virtual currency markets (CFTC 2018).[4] In March 2020, the CFTC issued its final interpretive guidance concerning

[3]The commission and federal courts frequently use the "investment contract" analysis to determine whether unique or novel instruments or arrangements, such as digital assets, are securities subject to federal securities laws. Specifically, based on the Howey Test formulated by the US Supreme Court, an "investment contract" exists when money is invested in a common enterprise with a reasonable expectation of profits to be derived from the efforts of others. Accordingly, whether a particular digital asset at the time of its offer or sale meets the Howey Test depends on the specific facts and circumstances of the case.

[4]CFTC Backgrounder on Oversight of and Approach to Virtual Currency Futures Markets.

the term "actual delivery"[5] for digital assets in order to inform the public of the commission's views when determining whether "actual delivery" has occurred in the context of retail commodity transactions involving virtual currencies.

Finally, FinCEN has classified cryptocurrencies as "money transmitters" subject to AML requirements. Specifically, in the final rule relating to money services businesses (2011),[6] FinCEN makes clear that persons (i.e. an individual, a corporation, a partnership, etc.) accepting and transmitting value that is a substitute for currency (e.g. virtual currency) are money transmitters[7] and, consequently, are required—just like any other money transmitter—to register with FinCEN as money services businesses (MSBs) and comply with the AML programme's recordkeeping, monitoring and reporting requirements. In March 2013, to address some of the concerns raised by the industry, FinCEN also issued interpretive guidance (hereafter, "the Guidance")[8] on the application of its regulations to transactions involving the acceptance of currency or funds and the transmission of "convertible virtual currencies" (CVCs). The Guidance describes what CVC are for purposes of FinCEN regulations and reminding the public that persons who are not exempt from MSB status and accept and transmit either real currency or anything of value that substitutes for currency, including virtual currency, are covered under the definition of money transmitter. Moreover, in May 2019, the FinCEN issued interpretive guidance to clarify for those who are subject to the Bank Secrecy Act how FinCEN regulations relating to money services businesses apply to certain business models involving money transmission

[5] As set forth in Section 2(c)(2)(D)(ii)(III)(aa) of the Commodity Exchange Act, pursuant to Section 742(a) of the Dodd-Frank Wall Street Reform and Consumer Protection Act.

[6] "2011 MSB Final Rule". Bank Secrecy Act Regulations—Definitions and Other Regulations Relating to Money Services Businesses, 76 FR 43585 (21 July 2011).

[7] FinCEN's regulations define the term "money transmitter" to include a "person that provides money transmission services" or "any other person engaged in the transfer of funds".

[8] The Guidance introduced the term "convertible virtual currency", defining it as "a type of virtual currency that either has an equivalent value as currency, or acts as a substitute for currency, and is therefore a type of 'value that substitutes for currency'". Thus, as money transmission involves the acceptance and transmission of value that is a substitute for currency by any means, transactions denominated in convertible virtual currencies will be subject to FinCEN regulations.

denominated in CVCs. This Guidance (2019) does not establish any new regulatory expectations or requirements but consolidates current FinCEN regulations and related administrative rulings and guidance issued since 2011. It applies these rules and interpretations to other common business models involving CVCs engaged in the same underlying patterns of activity.[9]

5.3.2 *EU Regulatory Approach to Cryptocurrencies*

Like the US, the EU has been seeking to boost the emerging cryptocurrency market while preventing misconduct and informing potential investors of risks. To this end, the EU's regulatory approach has involved addressing cryptocurrencies and especially crypto-players via the rules on money laundering and terrorist financing.

In 2016, the EC initiated legislative action to include "virtual currency exchange platforms" and "custodian wallet providers" under the scope of the Anti-Money Laundering Directive (AMLD) by proposing a fifth revision to the AMLD. The Fifth Anti-Money Laundering Directive (or AMLD5),[10] which amends the Fourth Anti-Money Laundering Directive, extends the definition of "obliged entities" to include virtual currency exchanges, defined as "providers engaged in exchange services between virtual currencies and fiat currencies", and custodian wallet providers, defined as "an entity that provides services to safeguard private cryptographic keys on behalf of its customers, to hold, store and transfer virtual currencies". Accordingly, virtual currency exchanges and custodian wallet providers have to comply with the same AML/CFT requirements as banks and other financial institutions: they must register with the national AML authorities, implement customer due diligence controls, monitor virtual currency transactions and report suspicious activity to government entities (Houben and Snyers 2020).

[9] For instance, it provides examples of how FinCEN's money transmission regulations apply to several common business models involving transactions in CVCs (e.g. P2P exchangers, CVC wallets, etc.) and how specific business models involving CVC transactions may be exempt from the definition of money transmission (e.g. CVC P2P trading platforms, dApp developer status, etc.).

[10] AMLD5 was published in the Official Journal of the European Union on 19 June 2018, and Member States had to transpose this new EU Directive in their national AML/CFT legislation by 10 January 2020.

Moreover, in its 2018 FinTech Action Plan, the EC requested that the European Supervisory Authorities (ESAs) assess the EU regulatory framework's suitability to ICOs and crypto-assets more generally in order to address regulatory concerns about investments in crypto-assets. To this end, while ESMA has focused on ICOs and assessed whether crypto-assets may qualify as "financial instruments" under Directive 2014/65/EU (MiFID), the EBA carried out a regulatory mapping of the applicability of current EU financial services law to crypto-assets within its sphere of responsibility by analysing the qualification of crypto-assets under the second Electronic Money Directive (Directive 2009/110/EC) and the second Payment Services Directive (Directive 2015/2366/EU).

First, ESMA analysed the legal qualification of crypto-assets under EU financial securities laws in line with its remit. To this end, ESMA surveyed[11] national competent authorities (NCAs) in the summer of 2018 to collect detailed feedback on the possible legal qualification of crypto-assets as financial instruments.[12] The outcome of the survey showed that, according to most NCAs, some crypto-assets (e.g. those with profit rights attached) could be deemed "transferable securities" and/or other types of financial instruments as defined under MiFID II (ESMA 2019). This means that some types of crypto-assets, provided they meet the relevant conditions, may qualify as transferable securities and/or other types of financial instruments and, therefore, should comply with the existing EU financial regulations.[13] However, the survey's results also showed that there were some variations across NCAs regarding

[11] The survey questions were designed to determine how a given Member State had transposed MiFID II into its national law and, based on that transposition, whether a sample set of six crypto-assets issued in an ICO qualified as "financial instruments" under their respective national laws.

[12] "Financial instruments" are defined in Article 4(1)(15) of MiFID II as those "instruments specified in Section C of Annex I". These include "transferable securities", "money market instruments", "units in collective investment undertakings" and various derivative instruments.

[13] Where crypto-assets qualify as transferable securities or other types of MiFID financial instruments, a full set of EU financial rules, including the Prospectus Directive, the Transparency Directive, MiFID II, the Market Abuse Directive, the Short Selling Regulation, the Central Securities Depositories Regulation and the Settlement Finality Directive, are likely to apply to their issuer and/or firms providing investment services/activities to those instruments.

the number of cases that would qualify, which depended on the relevant Member State's national definition of financial instruments. This means that the classification of a crypto-asset as a financial instrument is the responsibility of an individual NCA and will depend on the specific national implementation of EU law and the information and evidence provided to that NCA.[14] Accordingly, the same crypto-asset could be a financial instrument in one jurisdiction but not in another.

Second, the EBA has assessed whether crypto-assets may qualify as "electronic money"[15] within the second Electronic Money Directive (EMD2) or as "funds" under the second Payment Services Directive (PSD2), thereby complementing ESMA's analysis of whether crypto-assets may qualify as "financial instruments" according to the MiFID. The EBA (2019a) provides that, based on the specific characteristics of the crypto-asset, the asset may qualify as "electronic money" and, therefore, fall within the scope of the EMD2. For that reason, under Title II of EMD2, an electronic money institution requires authorisation to carry out activities involving electronic money, unless a limited network exemption applies in accordance with Article 9 of the same directive. Moreover, in the hypothesis that a firm proposes to use DLT to carry out a "payment service" as listed in Annex I to the PSD2 (e.g. the execution of payment transactions, including issuing "payment instruments" and/or acquiring payment transactions and money remittance) with a crypto-asset that qualifies as "electronic money", such an activity would fall within the scope of the PSD2 by virtue of being "funds".

Hence, the current perimeter of regulation in the EU is such that crypto-assets may, depending on their characteristics, qualify as financial instruments, electronic money or neither (EBA 2019a). Both ESMA and the EBA have identified many gaps and issues in the existing regulatory framework when applied to crypto-assets, as well as divergent approaches

[14] The results of the survey highlighted that, in the course of transposing MiFID into their national laws, the Member State NCAs did not define the term financial instrument in the same way. Some employed a restrictive list of examples to define transferable securities, while others used broader interpretations.

[15] A crypto-asset will qualify as electronic money as defined in point (2) of Article 2 of the EMD2 only if it satisfies each element of the definition: Electronic money means "electronically, including magnetically, stored monetary value as represented by a claim on the issuer which is issued on receipt of funds for the purpose of making payment transactions as defined in point 5 of Article 4 of [PSD2], and which is accepted by a natural or legal person other than the electronic money issuer".

to the regulation of these activities across the EU. Consequently, they have pointed out the need for further action and the importance of undertaking an EU-wide approach to address regulatory concerns about cryptocurrencies. In September 2020, the EC adopted a comprehensive package of legislative proposals for regulating crypto-assets by updating certain financial market rules for crypto-assets and creating a legal framework for regulatory sandboxes of financial supervisors in the EU to use blockchains in the trading and post-trading of securities. Specifically, for crypto-assets qualifying as "financial instruments", the commission proposed a pilot regime (i.e. a sandbox approach or controlled environment) for market infrastructures that wish to trade and settle transactions with financial instruments in crypto-asset form. This allows temporary derogations from existing rules so that regulators can gain experience on the use of DLT in market infrastructures while ensuring that they can deal with risks to investor protection, market integrity and financial stability. For other crypto-assets that do not qualify as "financial instruments", such as utility tokens or payment tokens, the EC has proposed a specific new framework that would replace all other EU rules and national rules currently governing the issuing, trading and storing of such crypto-assets. This Markets in Crypto-assets (MiCA) regulation aims to provide legal clarity and certainty to crypto-asset issuers and providers, covering not only entities issuing crypto-assets but also firms providing services around these crypto-assets (e.g. firms operating digital wallets), as well as cryptocurrency exchanges.

5.3.3 *Asia-Pacific Region's Regulatory Approach to Cryptocurrencies*

Countries in Asia have taken conflicting approaches to cryptocurrency regulation, with some aggressively prohibiting trading and others expressing support.

Japan has had relatively lenient cryptocurrency policies. It recognises Bitcoin and other cryptocurrencies as a form of money, although it recently increased scrutiny over exchanges' cybersecurity, AML and anti-fraud policies following a series of hacks (PWC 2018). In 2016, building on work by a study group in the Financial Services Agency (FSA), the government submitted a bill to the Diet (the Japanese parliament) to amend the Payment Services Act (PSA) and the Act on Prevention of Transfer of Criminal Proceeds, which defines cryptocurrencies, as well as the registration requirements for a virtual currency exchange service provider who engages in the sale, purchase and exchange of VCs.[16] Under the PSA, only business operators (persons) registered with the Prime Minister are allowed to engage in the virtual currency exchange service under the supervision of the FSA. Specifically, virtual currency exchange service providers are subject to national AML rules contained in the Act on Prevention of Transfer of Criminal Proceeds, including customer identification programme and suspicious transaction reporting.[17] Accordingly, they are obligated to check the identities of customers who open accounts, keep transaction records and notify the relevant authorities if a suspicious transaction is identified. A bill was approved in 2019 with proposed revisions to the PSA and the Financial Instruments and Exchange Acts (FIEA)—with specific regard to the introduction of the regulation governing crypto-assets derivative transactions—aimed at further strengthening the regulatory framework for virtual currencies[18] (Awataguchi and Nagase 2020). Regarding the regulation of ICOs, the FIEA revisions introduced the concept of "electronically recorded transferable rights" (ERTRs),[19] bringing tokens from the likes of ICOs and security token offerings under the regulatory oversight of the FIEA.[20]

By contrast, China has adopted a restrictive approach to cryptocurrencies by banning all ICOs and cracking down on trading platforms by not only banning national cryptocurrency exchanges but also restricting

[16] These amendments came into force on 1 April 2017.

[17] The act was amended in 2016 together with the PSA.

[18] Japan's FSA began enforcing the 2019 changes to the PSA and FIEA in May 2020.

[19] The concept refers to the rights set forth in Article 2, paragraph 2 of the FIAE that are represented by the proprietary value transferable by means of an electronic data processing system but limited only to proprietary values recorded in electronic devices or otherwise by electronic means.

[20] Under the FIAE, tokens issued in STOs are understood to constitute "collective investment scheme interests", which form when the following three requirements are met: (i) investors (i.e. right holders) invest or contribute cash or other assets to a business (ii) the cash or other assets contributed by investors are invested in the business, and (iii) investors have the right to receive dividends of profits or assets generated from investments in the business. Thus, tokens issued under STOs would constitute ERTRs if these three requirements are satisfied.

its residents' access to overseas platforms (PWC 2018; Holman and Stettner 2018). In 2013, Chinese regulatory bodies[21] issued the Notice on Preventing Bitcoin Risk (hereafter "the Notice"), providing that Bitcoin is not to be treated as a currency and stating that financial and payment institutions may not be involved in cryptocurrencies activities: they may not use Bitcoin to set prices for product or services, they may not buy or sell Bitcoins, they may not act as a market maker for Bitcoins, they may not directly or indirectly provide other Bitcoin-related services, and they may not accept Bitcoin or use Bitcoin as a payment tool. In September 2017, seven Chinese central government regulators jointly issued the Announcement on Preventing Risks from Initial Coin Offerings (ICO Rules), which bans all ICO activities in the country, branding them as "unauthorized and illegal public fundraising" and suspecting them "of involv[ement] in criminal activities such as illegal selling of tokens, illegal issuance of securities, illegal fundraising, financial fraud and pyramid schemes". In line with the 2013 Notice, the ICO Rules confirmed that the token or virtual currency used in coin offerings "does not have characteristics of money such as legal tender status and mandatory use, has no legal status equivalent to money, and cannot be circulated or used as currency in the market". Accordingly, it required that cryptocurrencies trading platforms cease exchanges of cryptocurrency for statutory currency. The ICO Rules also prohibited financial institutions and non-bank payment institutions from directly or indirectly providing services for ICOs and cryptocurrencies, including account opening, registration, trading, clearing and settlement for fundraising through coin offering/virtual currencies and so on. Nevertheless, it is worth noting that neither the Notice nor the ICO Rules ban Bitcoin or other cryptocurrencies from China; accordingly, there is no outright ban on individuals holding or transferring cryptocurrencies.

In Australia, the government has facilitated the growth of cryptocurrencies while ensuring that they are regulated (Reeves and Shen 2020), depending on the nature of the coin. According to the recently updated

[21] The People's Bank of China (PBOC), the Ministry of Industry and Information Technology (MIIT), the China Banking Regulatory Commission (CBRC), the China Securities Regulatory Commission (CSRC) and the China Insurance Regulatory Commission (CIRC).

regulatory guidance (INFO 225) (2017)[22] by the Australian Securities and Investments Commission (ASIC), the legal status of cryptocurrencies depends on how they are structured and the right attached to the coin or token, which ultimately determines the regulations with which an entity must comply. Specifically, depending on the circumstances, coins or tokens may constitute interests in managed investment schemes, securities or derivatives or fall into a category of more generally defined financial products—all of which are subject to Australia's financial services regulatory regime. Accordingly, entities offering coins or tokens that can be classified as financial products will need to comply with the regulatory requirements under the Corporations Act. These requirements generally include disclosure, registration, licensing and conduct obligations.[23] In 2017, the government passed the AML/CFT Amendment Act 2017, which went into force in April 2018 and brought cryptocurrencies and tokens under the purview of Australia's anti-money laundering and counter-terrorism financing regulatory regime. As a result, businesses supporting the exchange of cryptocurrency to fiat are classified as digital currency exchanges and are required to comply with the AML laws and regulations under the Anti-Money Laundering and Counter-Terrorism Financing Act 2006 (Holman and Stettner 2018). This implies that digital currency exchange providers are required to register with the Australian Transaction Reports and Analysis Centre (AUSTRAC) to operate, and they have to implement KYC processes to adequately verify their customers' identity, with ongoing obligations to monitor and report suspicious and threshold transactions. Exchange operators are also required to keep records relating to customer identification and transactions for seven years.

[22] Information Sheet 225 *Initial coin offerings and crypto-assets* (INFO 225), updated in May 2019.

[23] ICOs and crypto-assets that are not financial products, meaning that they are not regulated under the Corporations Act, may be still subject to other regulations and laws, including the Australian Consumer Law, which relates to the offering of services or products to Australian consumers and prohibits misleading or deceptive conduct in a range of circumstances, including in the context of marketing and advertising.

5.4 Regulatory Issues and Blockchain's Distributed Ledger Technology

As discussed in Chapter 3, banks can find themselves constrained when adopting blockchain's distributed ledger technology (DLT) to provide their services because of specific regulations on the banking industry or more general regulations that can limit its use in some banking processes and areas (ESMA 2016). First, a recurring argument concerns blockchain's compliance with existing data protection laws and the consequent privacy and security issues (e.g. when using blockchain to share customers' data during KYC processes). Data protection is a hot topic and a big challenge for those using new technologies such as blockchain; several regulations, such as the General Data Protection Regulation (GDPR) in the EU, are in place to ensure that customers' personal data are kept safe and used only for legitimate purposes (Finck 2019; PwC 2019). Another major issue is the uncertainty about the legal status of smart contracts (e.g. when used in trade finance), which generates some legal and regulatory issues related particularly to liability, jurisdiction, amendments and the voidability of contracts (Lauslahti et al. 2017; Gatteschi et al. 2018; Giudici and Adhami 2019). The problems mentioned above may render the operation of blockchain unlawful in some circumstances, thereby jeopardising its development. The EBA (2019b)[24] indicates some of the main challenges for the development of blockchain technology in EU banks: compliance with the existing EU regulatory framework (in particular, certain requirements of the GDPR), the uncertainties regarding the legal value of smart contracts and the lack of a clearly applicable jurisdiction, among others. Consequently, countries that are embracing blockchain's DLTs have started to face such regulatory issues in order to foster the development of the technology.

5.5 Regulators' Approach to the Adoption of Blockchain Technology

Authorities and regulators around the world are currently grappling with the adoption of blockchain's DLT in finance and, more specifically, the banking industry. The challenge they face is how best to

[24] In its Risk Assessment Report (2019), the EBA presented the status of the adoption of new technologies, such as blockchain, in EU banks.

apply technology-neutral regulations to ensure the broad adoption of blockchain technology, as well as compliance with existing regulatory frameworks, to ease the aforementioned problems. The following subsections give an overview of the different approaches that regulators have undertaken to embrace blockchain technology.

5.5.1 EU's Approach to Blockchain Technology

As mentioned above, a recurring issue regarding the adoption of blockchain technology is its compliance with existing data protection law. In the EU context, data protection enjoys the status of a fundamental right as set up in Article 8 of the Charter of Fundamental Rights, which provides that everyone has the right to protect their personal data. The GDPR,[25] which was ratified in 2016 and fully implemented in 2018, establishes a detailed legislative framework that harmonises data protection across the EU, strengthens a wide range of existing rights and establishes new ones for individuals. Specifically, the GDPR creates some obligations for data controllers, which are the entities determining the means and purpose of data processing, but also grants data subjects (i.e. the natural persons to whom the personal data relate) a set of rights that give them more control over how their personal data are processed and can be enforced against data controllers. Some of these provisions can generate tensions with the nature, technical specificities and governance design of blockchain technology (Lyons et al. 2019). In particular, a study by Finck (2019)[26] relates these tensions to two overarching factors. First, the GDPR is based on the underlying assumption that, in relation to each personal data point, there is at least one natural or legal person (i.e. the data controller) whom data subjects can contact to enforce their rights under EU data protection law. Conversely, blockchain seeks to achieve decentralisation by replacing a unitary actor with many different players, which makes it a challenge to allocate responsibility and accountability. Second, the GDPR is based on the assumption that data can be modified

[25] This regulation replaced the Data Protection Directive 95/46/EU, which had been adopted in 1995.

[26] This study was written by Dr Michèle Finck at the request of the Panel for the Future of Science and Technology (STOA) and managed by the Scientific Foresight Unit within the Directorate-General for Parliamentary Research Services (EPRS) of the Secretariat of the European Parliament.

or erased (i.e. the right to erasure)[27] where necessary to comply with legal requirements such as Articles 16 and 17 of the GDPR. This may not be technically feasible for the records/data stored on the blockchain (EBA 2019b). As discussed in Chapter 2, a key characteristic of blockchain technology is the irreversibility of records (immutability), which renders such modifications of data purposefully onerous. Although this study leads to the conclusion that the compatibility of blockchain with the GDPR should be assessed on a case-by-case basis,[28] it also shows that the interplay between the GDPR and blockchain is complex.

The aforementioned problems have not gone unnoticed by the EU authorities, which have recognised the challenges posed by the relationship between blockchain and the implementation of the GDPR and have started to address them. For instance, the European Parliament invited the European Data Protection Board (EDPB)[29] to issue guidelines and recommendations to ensure that blockchain technology complies with EU law. Although no guidelines had been issued by the time of this writing (October 2020), the EDPB had included blockchain as one of the possible topics to cover in its Work Program 2019/2020.

Another key topic concerns the use of smart contracts, whose legal and regulatory scope is still unclear. To date, no specific smart contract legal regimes have been created at the supranational or the Member State level, except for Italy, which has explicitly addressed regulatory issues concerning smart contracts by introducing a legal definition of smart

[27] The right to erasure ("right to be forgotten") provides that an individual can request that an organisation delete his/her personal data in some circumstances—e.g. where they are no longer necessary for the purposes for which they were originally collected or where the individual has withdrawn their consent.

[28] Specifically, Finck argues that it can be easier for private and permissioned blockchains to comply with these legal requirements than with public and permissionless blockchains, since it is easier to design private and permissioned blockchains in a manner that is compatible with EU data protection. As explained in previous chapters, this is because private blockchains are closed systems between pre-defined participants in which a single entity who sets the rules can have ownership and control over the whole blockchain, thus allowing the data to be treated in a compliant manner.

[29] The EDPB is an independent European body that contributes to the consistent application of data protection rules throughout the EU and promotes cooperation between the EU's data protection authorities.

contracts (and DLTs) and recognising their full legal validity and enforceability in the country.[30] Although no regulatory framework has been developed at the EU level, EU authorities have acknowledged the importance of promoting legal certainty for smart contracts and the need to further assess the risks related to their use. For instance, the EC commissioned a consortium[31] to analyse and evaluate the legal framework in the EU with regard to blockchain technology and its applications like smart contracts. The study identified several legal issues, including the application of contract law,[32] smart contracts' cross-border dimensions, the national legal requirements to have a written form of the contract and the application of consumer law, among others. However, the study's results point to the conclusion that no specific action has to be taken at this stage to address the aforementioned issues, suggesting the commission adopt a wait-and-see approach and develop regulatory guidance on specific issues concerning smart contracts (e.g. how exactly consumer protection law applies to smart contracts). Although such guidance has yet to be issued, one of the EC objectives is to propose a comprehensive pro-innovation legal framework in the area of smart contracts to promote legal certainty.

EU authorities have opened the door to blockchain's DLT, addressing several regulatory concerns surrounding its adoption. Nevertheless, the consideration above has led to the conclusion that further action is needed to generate more legal certainty since a clear regulatory regime is key to allowing a wider adoption of blockchain technology in compliance with existing EU laws.

5.5.2 US Approach to Blockchain Technology

Unlike the EU, which is seeking to develop a uniform regulatory framework across the union, the US regulatory framework on blockchain is

[30] Article 8-ter, Law 11 February 2019, no 12 (Simplification Law). According to the law, smart contracts satisfy the requirement of written form prior computerised identification of interested parties by means of a process with requirements established by the Digital Italy Agency with guidelines; the guidelines must be adopted within 90 days from the entry into force of the conversion law of this Legislative Decree. However, the Agid has yet to issue any such guidelines.

[31] The reference is to the "Study on Blockchains: legal, governance and interoperability aspects (SMART 2018/0038)" carried out by the Spark Legal Network, Michèle Finck, Tech4i2 and Datarella (together also referred to as the Consortium).

[32] Contract law applies to smart contracts provided that they qualify as legal contracts.

fragmented, with each state adopting a different approach: some states have enacted laws allowing the use of blockchain technology and its applications in several contexts, while others have only started to evaluate its impact and their ability to leverage the technology.

For instance, regarding the relationship between blockchain and data protection laws, it is worth noting that the US has not implemented a comprehensive federal data protection framework but relies instead on state and sector-specific privacy and data security laws and regulations. There is not one piece of data protection legislation but several laws enacted at both the federal (e.g. the Federal Trade Commission Act) and the state level to protect US residents' personal data (Chabinsky and Pittman 2020), which often applies to specific industry sectors (e.g. the Gramm Leach Bliley Act governing the protection of personal information in the hands of banks, insurance companies and other companies in the financial services industry). As a result, there is also not one single regulatory approach to the relationship between blockchain and data protection in the US. An example worth mentioning comes from the state of California, which addresses the relationship between blockchain and the state-level data protection law, the California Consumer Privacy Act (CCPA) (Cal. Civil Code § 1798.100 et seq.) became effective in January 2020.[33] In 2018, an assembly bill led to the creation of a blockchain technology working group to evaluate the uses, risks, benefits and legal implications of blockchain and to recommend amendments to existing laws that may be impacted by blockchain.[34] With specific regard to data privacy legislation, the study's main conclusion was that California's privacy laws need not be amended to enable the adoption of blockchain technologies and use cases. However, it also suggested continuously monitoring pending legislation for potential new issues with blockchain applications related to the protection of individuals' privacy that are not addressed by the existing regulatory framework and to take further action (e.g. by issuing guidance on how to deploy blockchain in

[33] Similarly to the GDPR, the California Consumer Privacy Act of 2018 (CCPA) gives consumers more control over the information that businesses collect about them by granting new privacy rights to California consumers, including the right to know which personal information a business collects about them and how it is used and shared, the right to delete personal information collected about them (with some exceptions) etc.

[34] AB 2658 (Calderon, Chapter 875, Statutes of 2018, G.C. 11546.9) required that the Secretary of the Government Operations Agency appoint a blockchain technology working group and chairperson by 1 July 2019.

a manner that comports with California privacy laws) to generate more legal certainty on the argument.

Concerning the use of smart contracts, the main argument is that they are already enforceable under general federal contract law principles in the United States. According to a study by the Chamber of Digital Commerce (2018), insofar as smart contract technology is used in the terms of a legal contract, existing law and traditional legal analysis already apply and ensure efficacy. Its study demonstrates that existing law in the form of the Electronic Signatures in Global and National Commerce Act ("ESIGN Act") and the Uniform Electronic Transactions Act ("UETA")[35] currently provide a sufficient legal basis for smart contracts using the terms of a legal contract to be regarded as legally binding once it is electronically signed. However, although there are strong arguments that existing state laws already provide a sound basis for the enforceability of smart contracts, several states (e.g. Arizona, Tennessee, Vermont, etc.) have also legislated in this respect. Some states have amended their laws to allow for the enforceability of blockchain-based contracts, and many other states have enacted laws that recognise blockchain technology and blockchain-based legal instruments. Some examples include the state of Arizona, which, in 2017, amended its version of the UETA, the Arizona Electronic Transaction Act (AETA), to legally recognise blockchain-secured records, signatures and smart contracts: "a contract relating to a transaction may not be denied legal effect, validity or enforceability solely because that contract contains a smart contract term".[36] More recently, in January 2020, the state of Illinois passed the Blockchain Technology Act (BTA), a law directly targeting blockchain technology and smart contract enforceability.

Many other states have also enacted legislation on this issue. Nevertheless, since existent laws already provide a sufficient legal foundation for the enforcement of these types of agreements, many parties (Chamber of

[35] The UETA aims to remove legal barriers that prevented the effective use of electronic media by making electronic records and signatures equal to paper records and wet signatures. Like the UETA, the ESIGN establishes legal parity between electronic records and signatures and their paper and ink counterparts.

[36] HB 2417. An Act amending Section 44-7003, Arizona revised statutes; amending Title 44, Chapter 26, Arizona revised statutes, by adding Article 5; relating to electronic transactions.

Digital Commerce 2018; Levi et al. 2020) argue that additional legislation could create inconsistent state laws, confuse the marketplace and potentially hinder innovation. For instance, as Levi et al. (2020) suggest, as a growing number of states are adopting different definitions for the same terms, the potential for disputes between parties relying on smart contracts increases, and the determination of which state's law governs becomes more important. This points to the need for a uniform approach to regulate blockchain technology and smart contracts in order to avoid conflicting laws that may jeopardise the development of the technology.

5.5.3 *Asian-Pacific Countries' Approach to Blockchain Technology*

Other jurisdictions around the world have also started to take steps to implement regulations in relation to the use and development of blockchain's DLTs (Ellul et al. 2020).

Despite the ban on ICOs and cryptocurrency exchanges (see subsection 5.3.3), China has been increasingly involved in the blockchain arena to advance innovation across the country. The People's Bank of China (PBOC) and other government agencies have consistently shown great enthusiasm for the application of blockchain technology and have undertaken several initiatives in terms of technical implementation and regulatory reforms to support research and development in this sector. For instance, in January 2019, the Cyberspace Administration of China (CAC)—China's cyberspace information regulator—released its Administrative Provisions on Blockchain Information Services (Blockchain Provisions), a set of rules governing blockchain-based information services that set out certain requirements for blockchain service providers[37] to ensure compliance with applicable laws and regulations in the country (Zhang 2019). With specific regard to the financial services industry, in February 2020, the PBOC released the financial industry standard "JR/T 0184—2020 Financial Distributed Ledger Technology Security Specification" to provide a common base standard for the development of financial services using DLTs. Specifically, this standard aims to help financial institutions to deploy and maintain systems in accordance with the relevant security requirements and provide business assurance capability and information

[37] The Blockchain Provisions apply to blockchain information services in China, which are defined as services providing information to the public through websites or applications based on blockchain technology or systems.

security risk constraint capability for the large-scale application of DLT. To this end, it addresses various aspects of such systems, including policy and technical requirements, privacy protection principles and regulatory issues on smart contracts.

The Japanese government has also embraced blockchain technology and undertaken several initiatives to encourage its use (González 2018). Japanese authorities have addressed blockchain-related regulatory issues. However, no blockchain-specific regulatory framework currently exists in Japan, nor have any specific laws been amended to address the regulatory concerns deriving from the adoption of blockchain technology. Among the different initiatives, it is worth mentioning the interest of Japanese authorities in implementing regulatory sandboxes to promote the development and usage of blockchain technology and other new technologies (e.g. AI, IoT and big data). For instance, in June 2018, a cross-governmental one-stop desk for a regulatory sandbox scheme in Japan was established within the Japan Economic Revitalization Bureau to enable companies that apply and receive approval to carry out (under certain conditions) a demonstration of their projects, even if such activities are not yet covered under current laws and regulations (Kawai and Sasaki 2020). The FSA also established its own sandboxes on different areas in fintech and, in 2017, launched the "FinTech PoC (Proof-of-Concept) Hub". With specific regard to blockchain technology, the experiment concerns KYC information sharing via blockchain, which consisted of using blockchain to jointly implement a customer identity verification system for financial institutions. These regulatory sandboxes allow Japanese regulators to stay abreast of new business ideas and products and to learn where they might need to update or fill gaps in existing regulatory frameworks (González 2018).

In Australia, there are currently no specific regulations dealing with blockchain's DLT (Reeves and Shen 2020). However, the country's government agencies have sought to clarify the regulatory issues affecting the implementation and use of blockchain, particularly in the financial sector. To outline its regulatory framework, the ASIC released an information sheet (INFO 219—Evaluating distributed ledger technology) in March 2017 for both existing licensees and start-up businesses considering operating market infrastructure or providing financial or consumer credit services using DLT. In this information sheet, the ASIC reasserted its "technology-neutral approach" to regulation and claimed that businesses using blockchain are subject to the compliance requirements that currently exist under the applicable licensing regime.[38] Moreover, according to the information sheet, the existing regulatory framework can accommodate the DLT use cases that have been observed. The ASIC has also established an Innovation Hub designed to help Australian fintech start-ups, including blockchain-related businesses, to navigate Australia's regulatory system. Furthermore, the Australian government has engaged with industry and researchers to develop a National Blockchain Roadmap focused on several policy areas such as regulation, skill building, investment and international competitiveness and collaboration. This roadmap, published in February 2020, identifies a number of common regulatory issues across a large number of use cases[39] and lays out a strategy for governments, industry and researchers to tackle them by indicating some potential initiatives for the future.

5.6 Conclusions

This chapter discussed the main regulatory issues related to the adoption of blockchain technology and its applications, and it provided an overview of how regulators and authorities around the world are tackling them.

First, it is important to distinguish between regulatory issues deriving from cryptocurrencies and those that result from banks adopting blockchain's DLT to provide their services. The regulatory concerns around cryptocurrencies relate particularly to their use for illicit activities (e.g. fraud and manipulation, tax evasion, money laundering, etc.). Many countries have tried to regulate cryptocurrencies by taking different approaches: some have recognised cryptocurrencies and regulated their scope; others have prohibited them altogether; and still others have not taken any action at all. Although the initiatives that regulators have undertaken represent an important step to address cryptocurrencies risks, some concerns remain. As emphasised by the FSB (2019a), the diversity of national regulatory responses and the consequent gaps, overlaps and conflicts that may occur among them may produce asymmetries across

[38] The regulatory framework requires entities to have adequate technological resources and risk management arrangements, as well as the necessary human resources and organisational competence.

[39] Including privacy (a key regulatory challenge for privacy and blockchain systems in Australia is the need to comply with the Privacy Act 1988), security of blockchain systems, integrity of data and the legal status of smart contracts.

jurisdictions that can create significant loopholes for criminals and terrorists to abuse. This calls for an appropriate multilateral response and more coordination among regulators. International bodies are actively working on a variety of issues relating to crypto-assets, including investor and consumer protection, market integrity, bank exposures, AML/CFT, etc., to provide a uniform approach.[40]

Second, the regulatory issues around blockchain's DLT concern, in particular, its compliance with some existing laws (e.g. data protection laws) and the legal uncertainty surrounding smart contracts, both of which are significant barriers to blockchain adoption. Several regulatory initiatives have been undertaken to assess the need for new regulations or a modification of existing ones. Although some conflicts have been identified between existing regulatory framework and blockchain, the central argument, in many cases, is that the current legal framework can accommodate blockchain technology (particularly private blockchains) and its applications. However, certain issues still need to be addressed. In particular, more legal certainty is needed to reconcile existing laws (e.g. some aspects of data privacy laws) with blockchain, which does not necessarily imply changes to existing rules but at least guidance from the relevant authorities. Moreover, greater coordination among jurisdictions to provide a uniform approach to regulating blockchain is crucial to avoid conflicting laws that may jeopardise the adoption of blockchain in several contexts (e.g. the use of smart contracts in trade finance).

Although a great deal has been accomplished over the past few years, further action is still needed to provide the clear regulatory framework that is necessary to enable blockchain to flourish and ensure consumer and other stakeholder protections in the banking (and, more generally, the financial) industry.

[40] For instance, the Financial Action Task Force (FATF) has issued global, binding standards to prevent the misuse of virtual assets for money laundering and terrorist financing in order to ensure that virtual assets are treated fairly by applying the same safeguards as the financial sector.

References

ASIC. (2017). *INFO 219—Evaluating distributed ledger technology*. Available at: https://asic.gov.au/regulatory-resources/digital-transformation/evaluating-distributed-ledger-technology/.

ASIC. (2017). INFO 225—*Initial coin offerings and crypto-assets*. Available at: https://asic.gov.au/regulatory-resources/digital-transformation/initial-coin-offerings-and-crypto-assets/.

Assembly Bill No. 2658, Chapter 875. Available at: https://leginfo.legislature.ca.gov/faces/billTextClient.xhtml?bill_id=201720180AB2658.

Australian Government. (2017). *Anti-money laundering and counter-terrorism financing amendment act 2017*. Available at: https://www.legislation.gov.au/Details/C2017A00130.

Australian Government. (2020). *National blockchain roadmap. Progressing towards a blockchain-empowered future*. Available at: https://www.industry.gov.au/sites/default/files/2020-02/national-blockchain-roadmap.pdf.

Awataguchi & Nagase. (2020). *Blockchain & cryptocurrency regulation 2020* (Japan Chapter). Available at: https://www.globallegalinsights.com/practice-areas/blockchain-laws-and-regulations/japan.

Beauchamp, T. W., Wink, S. P., & Hawkins, S. (2019). *Crypto-asset trading platforms: A regulatory trip around the world*. GLI—Fintech 2019, First Edition. Available at: https://www.lw.com/thoughtLeadership/crypto-asset-trading-platforms-regulatory-trip-around-the-world.

CFTC. (2018). *CFTC backgrounder on oversight of and approach to virtual currency futures markets*. Available at: https://www.cftc.gov/sites/default/files/idc/groups/public/@newsroom/documents/file/backgrounder_virtualcurrency01.pdf.

CFTC. (2020). *Final interpretive guidance on actual Delivery for digital assets*. Available at: https://www.cftc.gov/PressRoom/PressReleases/8139-20.

Chabinsky & Pittman. (2020). *USA: Data protection laws and regulations 2020*. Available at: https://iclg.com/practice-areas/data-protection-laws-and-regulations/usa.

Chamber of Digital Commerce. (2018). *Smart contracts: Is the law ready?*. Available at: https://digitalchamber.s3.amazonaws.com/Smart-Contracts-Whitepaper-WEB.pdf.

Congress. (2020). *H.R.6154—Crypto-Currency Act of 2020*. Available at: https://www.congress.gov/bill/116th-congress/house-bill/6154/text?r=6&s=1.

EBA. (2019a). *Report with advice for the European Commission on crypto-assets*. Available at: https://eba.europa.eu/sites/default/documents/files/documents/10180/2545547/67493daa-85a8-4429-aa91-e9a5ed880684/EBA%20Report%20on%20crypto%20assets.pdf.

EBA. (2019b). *Risk assessment of the European banking system*, November 2019. Available at: https://eba.europa.eu/sites/default/documents/files/document_library/Risk%20Analysis%20and%20Data/EU%20Wide%20Transparency%20Exercise/2019/Transparency%20exercise%20documents/Risk_Assessment_Report_November_2019.PDF.

EBA. (2020). *EBA response EC consultation on the digital finance strategy/action plan*. Available at: https://eba.europa.eu/sites/default/documents/files/document_library/About%20Us/Missions%20and%20tasks/Correspondence%20with%20EU%20institutions/2020/886668/EBA%20Response%20to%20EC%20DFS%20consultation%20260620.pdf.

EC. (2016). Working document Impact Assessment, Accompanying the document Proposal for a Directive of the European Parliament and the Council amending Directive (EU) 2015/849 on the prevention of the use of the financial system for the purposes of money laundering or terrorist financing and amending Directive 2009/101/EC. Available at: https://eur-lex.europa.eu/legal-content/EN/TXT/PDF/?uri=CELEX:52016SC0223&from=EN.

EC. (2018). *FinTech action plan: For a more competitive and innovative European financial sector*. Available at: https://ec.europa.eu/info/sites/info/files/180308-action-plan-fintech_en.pdf.

EC. (2020). *Digital Finance Package: Commission sets out new, ambitious approach to encourage responsible innovation to benefit consumers and businesses*. Available at: https://ec.europa.eu/commission/presscorner/detail/en/IP_20_1684.

ECB. (2019). *Crypto-assets: Implications for financial stability, monetary policy, and payments and market infrastructures*. Occasional Paper Series. No 223/May 2019. Available at: https://www.ecb.europa.eu/pub/pdf/scpops/ecb.op223~3ce14e986c.en.pdf?a31360223fb32f0e50a82ce649a8b7fc.

EC Spark Legal Network, Finck, M., Tech4i2, & Datarella. (2018). *Study on blockchains—Legal, governance and interoperability aspects (SMART 2018/0038)*. Available at: https://ec.europa.eu/digital-single-market/en/news/study-blockchains-legal-governance-and-interoperability-aspects-smart-20180038.

EDPB. (2019). *Work program 2019/2020*. Available at: https://edpb.europa.eu/sites/edpb/files/files/file1/edpb-2019-02-12plen-2.1edpb_work_program_en.pdf.

Ellul, J., Galea, J., Ganado, M., Mccarthy, S., & Pace, G. J. (2020). Regulating blockchain, DLT and smart contracts: A technology regulator's perspective. In *ERA Forum* (Vol. 21, No. 2, pp. 209–220). Springer Berlin Heidelberg.

ESMA. (2016). *Discussion paper. The distributed ledger technology applied to securities markets*. Available at: https://www.esma.europa.eu/sites/default/files/library/2016-773_dp_dlt.pdf.

ESMA. (2019). *Advice initial coin offerings and crypto-assets*. Available at: https://www.esma.europa.eu/sites/default/files/library/esma50-157-1391_crypto_advice.pdf.

European Parliament. (2018). Directive (EU) 2018/843 of the European Parliament and of the Council of 30 May 2018 amending Directive (EU) 2015/849 on the prevention of the use of the financial system for the purposes of money laundering or terrorist financing, and amending Directives 2009/138/EC and 2013/36/EU. Available at: https://eur-lex.europa.eu/legal-content/EN/TXT/PDF/?uri=CELEX:32018L0843&from=EN.

European Parliament and the Council. (2016). Regulation (EU) 2016/679 of the European Parliament and of the Council of 27 April 2016 on the protection of natural persons with regard to the processing of personal data and on the free movement of such data, and repealing Directive 95/46/EC (General Data Protection Regulation). Available at: https://eur-lex.europa.eu/legal-content/EN/TXT/PDF/?uri=CELEX:32016R0679&from=EN.

FINCEN. (2011). *2011 MSB Final Rule. Bank secrecy act regulations—Definitions and other regulations relating to money services businesses*, 76 FR 43585. Available at: https://www.federalregister.gov/documents/2011/07/21/2011-18309/bank-secrecy-act-regulations-definitions-and-other-regulations-relating-to-money-services-businesses.

FINCEN. (2013). *Application of FinCEN's regulations to persons administering, exchanging, or using virtual currencies*. Available at: https://www.fincen.gov/sites/default/files/shared/FIN-2013-G001.pdf.

FINCEN. (2019). *Application of FinCEN's regulations to certain business models involving convertible virtual currencies*. Available at: https://www.fincen.gov/sites/default/files/2019-05/FinCEN%20Guidance%20CVC%20FINAL%20508.pdf.

Finck. (2019). *Blockchain and the general data Protection regulation. Can distributed ledgers be squared with European data protection law?*. Available at: https://www.europarl.europa.eu/RegData/etudes/STUD/2019/634445/EPRS_STU(2019)634445_EN.pdf.

French T., & Stettner B. (2019). *Anti-Money laundering regulation of cryptocurrency: U.S. and global approaches*. Allen & Overy, LLP.

FSB. (2019a). *Crypto-assets: Work underway, regulatory approaches and potential gaps*. Available at: https://www.fsb.org/wp-content/uploads/P310519.pdf.

FSB. (2019b). *Decentralised financial technologies. Report on financial stability, regulatory and governance implications*. Available at: https://www.fsb.org/wp-content/uploads/P060619.pdf.

Gatteschi, V., Lamberti, F., Demartini, C., Pranteda, C., & Santamaría, V. (2018). To blockchain or not to blockchain: That is the question. *IT Professional*, *20*(2), 62–74. https://doi.org/10.1109/MITP.2018.021921652.

Giudici, G., & Adhami, S. (2019). The impact of governance signals on ICO fundraising success. *Journal of Industrial and Business Economics, 46*(2), 283–312.

González, M. (2018). *Blockchain in Japan. EU-Japan centre for industrial cooperation*. Available at: https://www.eu-japan.eu/sites/default/files/publications/docs/blockchaininjapan-martagonzalez.pdf.

Holman & Stettner. (2018). *Anti-money laundering regulation of cryptocurrency: U.S. and Global Approaches*. Allen & Overy, LLP.

Houben & Snyers. (2020). *Crypto-assets key developments, regulatory concerns and responses*. Available at: https://www.europarl.europa.eu/RegData/etudes/STUD/2020/648779/IPOL_STU(2020)648779_EN.pdf.

Houben, R., & Snyers, A. (2018). *Cryptocurrencies and blockchain: Legal context and implications for financial crime, money laundering and tax Evasion*, European Parliament. Available at: https://www.europarl.europa.eu/cmsdata/150761/TAX3%20Study%20on%20cryptocurrencies%20and%20blockchain.pdf.

Kawai & Sasaki. (2020). *Japan: Fintech laws and regulations 2020*. ICLG. Available at: https://iclg.com/practice-areas/fintech-laws-and-regulations/japan.

Lauslahti, K., Mattila, J., & Seppala, T. (2017). Smart contracts–How will blockchain technology affect contractual practices?. *Etla Reports* (68).

Levi, S., Vasile, C., & Neal, M. (2020). *Blockchain & cryptocurrency regulation 2021. 12 Legal issues surrounding the use of smart contracts*. Global legal insights. Available at: https://www.globallegalinsights.com/practice-areas/blockchain-laws-and-regulations/12-legal-issues-surrounding-the-use-of-smart-contracts.

Lucking, D., & Aravind, V. (2020). *Cryptocurrency as a commodity: The CFTC's Regulatory Framework*. GLI—Fintech 2020, Second Edition. Allen & Overy LLP.

Lyons, T., Courcelas, L., & Timsit, K. (2019). *Legal and regulatory framework of blockchains and smart contracts*. Thematic Report. European Union Blockchain Observatory & Forum 2019. Available at: https://www.eublockchainforum.eu/sites/default/files/reports/report_legal_v1.0.pdf.

People's Republic of China. (2020). *Financial industry standards financial distributed ledger technology security specification 2020*. Available at: https://www.chinesestandard.net/PDF/English.aspx/JRT0184-2020.

PWC. (2018). *Carving up crypto: Regulators begin to find their footing*. Available at: https://www.pwc.com/us/en/financial-services/regulatory-services/publications/assets/cryptocurrency.pdf.

PWC. (2019). *Data protection within new technologies: blockchain Is your personal data secure when processed on a blockchain?* Available at: https://www.pwc.ch/en/publications/2019/Data%20protection%20within%20new%20technologies_EN-web.pdf.

Reeves & Shen. (2020). *Blockchain & cryptocurrency regulation 2021|Australia*. Global legal insights, third edition. Available at: https://www.globallegalinsights.com/practice-areas/blockchain-laws-and-regulations/australia.

SEC. (2017). *Statement on cryptocurrencies and initial coin offerings*. Available at: https://www.sec.gov/news/public-statement/statement-clayton-2017-12-11.

SEC. (2018). *Statement on potentially unlawful online platforms for trading digital assets*. Available at: https://www.sec.gov/news/public-statement/enforcement-tm-statement-potentially-unlawful-online-platforms-trading.

SEC. Strategic Hub for Innovation and Financial Technology. (2019). *Framework for "investment contract" analysis of digital assets*. Available at: https://www.sec.gov/files/dlt-framework.pdf.

State of Arizona House of Representatives. (2017). HB 2417. An Act amending section 44–7003, Arizona revised statutes; amending Title 44, Chapter 26, Arizona revised statutes, by adding Article 5; relating to electronic transactions. Available at: https://legiscan.com/AZ/text/HB2417/id/1497439/Arizona-2017-HB2417-Introduced.html.

State of California, Department of Justice. (2018). *California consumer privacy act of 2018*. Available at: http://leginfo.legislature.ca.gov/faces/codes_displayText.xhtml?division=3.&part=4.&lawCode=CIV&title=1.81.5.

Zhang, L. (2019). *China: Rules on blockchain-based information services issued requiring authentication of users' real identities*. Available at: https://www.loc.gov/law/foreign-news/article/china-rules-on-blockchain-based-information-services-issued-requiring-authentication-of-users-real-identities/.

CHAPTER 6

Final Remarks

Abstract This chapter provides a concluding discussion of the study. It offers remarks on the main topics of the book and summarises the potential implications of blockchain technology for traditional banking business models. Finally, it identifies avenues for future research on the topic.

Keyword Blockchain · Distributed ledger technology · Banking

The banking industry is in the midst of major changes, and banks are facing several challenges. On the one hand, recent advances in technologies have had a significant impact on the expectations and behaviours of consumers, who are now demanding better-quality and more customised services and products. At the same time, new technologies are increasing competition in the industry, opening the doors to many new entrants (e.g. fintech firms and technology providers) seeking to offer financial services in innovative ways and provide a better user experience. On the other hand, new technologies are enabling banks to improve the efficiency of the processes underlying their offer of financial services. In this regard, new technologies can be instrumental in improving the quality of the services being offered to clients and ensure that they have a competitive edge.

P. Martino, *Blockchain and Banking*,
https://doi.org/10.1007/978-3-030-70970-9_6

In this environment, an innovation that is relevant for the banking industry is blockchain technology—a decentralised and distributed ledger that is constantly updated and allows for the recording of transactions and the tracking of assets in a given network (Swan 2015; Crosby et al. 2016; Walport 2016). It started as the technology underlying Bitcoin (Nakamoto 2008)—that is, first-generation blockchain (Blockchain 1.0.), which has been used to allow the recording of Bitcoin (and other cryptocurrencies) transactions—and has become a tool facilitating the process of recording any transaction type and tracking the movement of any asset. These uses have made it applicable to multiple areas in the form of second-generation blockchain (Blockchain 2.0) onwards (Ulieru 2016; Iansiti and Lakhani 2017; Tapscott and Tapscott 2017). Specifically, blockchain represents a break and a more efficient alternative from the centralised data repositories that have historically been used to support transaction processing (Yermack 2017): by combining several computer technologies, including distributed data storage, point-to-point transmission, consensus mechanisms and cryptography functions, blockchain can solve the problems of traditional databases (i.e. centralised systems). Blockchain allows fast, low-cost and secure transactions without the need for third parties.

Thanks to the characteristics of the underlying technology, blockchain has been widely acknowledged as a disruptive force in the financial sector and a key source of future financial market innovation because it undermines the traditional business models still used in many financial service transactions. Concerning the banking industry, in particular, numerous studies (e.g. MacDonald et al. 2016; Buitenhek 2016; Guo and Liang 2016; Peters and Panayi 2016; Yermack 2019; Stulz 2019) argue that blockchain can create new opportunities for banks and pose new threats to their business. In this regard, this study underscores the importance of differentiating between the various types and uses of blockchain technology.

First-generation blockchain—i.e. blockchain used to launch cryptocurrencies (usually public blockchains)—poses a threat to banks because blockchain and cryptocurrencies (like Bitcoin) are tools that can be used to disintermediate banks. Specifically, blockchain linked to cryptocurrencies enables new players (e.g. blockchain-based start-ups) to enter the market and offer products and services that have traditionally been banking products, as well as new and innovative ones, at a lower price, thereby increasing competition in the banking industry. This may cause banks to lose their market shares and, consequently, jeopardises their profitability. Conversely, second-generation blockchain—i.e. the adoption of the distributed ledger technology (DLT) of blockchain that provides banking services (usually private blockchains)—gives banks an opportunity since the technology can improve the quality of the services they offer their clients. In particular, by automating such processes and eliminating the parties involved in the operations, blockchain's DLT can enhance the efficiency of middle and back-office processes and, consequently, improve the products and services the banks offer their customers. Activities like lending, payments, trade finance and capital markets are the main banking areas that may benefit from adopting the technology, which can cut costs and increase transaction speeds. In addition, as discussed in Chapter 3, blockchain can allow banks to create new product and services and reach new potential customers (i.e. unbanked and underbanked populations), thus generating new and potentially important revenue streams. Through these three channels (i.e. efficiency improvements, product innovation and new market segments), blockchain technology can positively affect banks' profitability and represent an important source of competitive edge.

Banks are compelled to rethink their operations, business models and strategies to cope with the challenges mentioned above. This book provides new insights on the developments, trends and challenges of using blockchain in the banking industry. More specifically, it outlines the potential impact of blockchain's DLT on the traditional banking business model and the current undertaking by banks to embrace the technology.

Building on the framework of the Business Model Canvas by Osterwalder and Pigneur (2010), this study shows that blockchain's potential impact on banks' business models could be broad, with all the elements of a bank's business model significantly affected. As discussed in Chapter 4, blockchain can enable banks to offer their customers a new value proposition, namely providing traditional products and services more efficiently and creating and offering new ones that are not necessarily associated with traditional banking products but are tailored to meet customers' individual needs. For this reason, innovation will become a central element of a bank's strategy. Moreover, the technology can allow banks to open new market segments, thereby reaching a multitude of new potential customers. This will require banks to rethink their key internal resources and activities, as well as their partnerships, to make the new value proposition possible. First, banks will need to move outside of their traditional resources to improve their ability to deal with and leverage the technology in order to foster innovative solutions. In particular, human resources capable of understanding the technology and translate it into costs and economy of scale (e.g. blockchain experts, technologists, IT experts, etc.), as well as resources that can help to develop and exploit the vast and diversified quantity of information recorded in the distributed ledger (e.g. data scientists), will be key enablers of the new business models. At the same time, activities like *data analytics, research & development* and *customer relationship management* will be major factors driving innovation in banks and, in this way, become more valuable than they ever were before. In this regard, collaboration with other financial institutions, technology firms (e.g. blockchain-based start-ups) and universities will be crucial for banks to acquire particular resources or perform certain activities.

Hence, in line with previous studies (e.g. Nowinski and Kozma 2017; Morkunas et al. 2019; Rajnak and Puschmann 2020), this study suggests that blockchain can change the status quo and lead to new business models in banking. To date, however, it has been difficult to assess how and to what extent blockchain can affect the traditional banking business model.

Although blockchain continues to develop at a rapid pace, with numerous large banks investing and experimenting with the technology, recent evidence (Bank of Italy 2019; EBA 2019) shows that most blockchain projects in banks are still in the development phase. Moreover, some restrictions on the widespread adoption of blockchain persist and have to be addressed. This relates particularly to the interoperability among different types of blockchains and compliance with existing regulatory frameworks. In this regard, it is worth pointing out that much has been done over the years to face such challenges. As discussed in Chapter 5, regulators and authorities around the world have been actively assessing compatibility with the current regulatory framework and identifying any regulatory "gaps" and potential risks. To this end, numerous initiatives, including the revision of existing rules and/or the introduction of new ones, have been undertaken to promote the development of the technology in compliance with the existing regulatory framework. At the same time, banks are actively collaborating with each other and with other stakeholders (governments, universities, etc.) to promote the development of the technology and its applications in financial services. Nevertheless, it is worth noting that further action is still needed to enable blockchain to flourish.

With the technology advancing at an accelerated pace, academic research should also offer an important contribution to the understanding of the technology and the evaluation of its possible uses in the banking sector. Despite the growing number of studies on blockchain technology, the literature on blockchain in banking is still in its infancy, with the majority of studies being conceptual. Therefore, this study indicates the need for further research on this topic. First, a deeper investigation of blockchain projects in banks would be needed to fully understand the implications of the technology for banking business models. For instance, future studies could build on the framework of the Business Model Canvas to explore whether blockchain projects lead to a revision of existing business models (e.g. by optimising existing processes to increase overall efficiency and the quality of products and services) or change it completely (e.g. by offering a new value proposition such as the development of new products and services). Moreover, with more projects moving from the pilot stage to the production phase, it will be interesting to provide empirical evidence about the true benefits that blockchain technology may provide for banks and their profitability. This is essential to understand which banking areas can benefit from the adoption of blockchain and to identify which (internal and external) factors can determine whether the implementation of the technology in banks is successful or not. In turn, this will provide important insights into the ways in which banks (can) tackle the challenges of blockchain technology.

References

Bank of Italy. (2019). *Indagine fintech nel sistema finanziario italiano*. Available at: https://www.bancaditalia.it/compiti/vigilanza/analisi-sistema/approfondimenti-banche-int/Allegato_2_Indagine_Fintech.pdf.

Buitenhek, M. (2016). Understanding and applying blockchain technology in banking: Evolution or revolution? *Journal of Digital Banking, 1*(2), 111–119.

Crosby, M., Pattanayak, P., Verma, S., & Kalyanaraman, V. (2016). BlockChain technology: Beyond Bitcoin. *Applied Innovation Review, 71*(2), 6–10.

EBA. (2019). *Risk assessment of the European Banking System*, November 2019. Available at: https://eba.europa.eu/sites/default/documents/files/document_library/Risk%20Analysis%20and%20Data/EU%20Wide%20Transparency%20Exercise/2019/Transparency%20exercise%20documents/Risk_Assessment_Report_November_2019.PDF.

Guo, Y., & Liang, C. (2016). Blockchain application and outlook in the banking industry. *Financial Innovation, 2*(1), 24.

Iansiti, M., & Lakhani, K. R. (2017). The truth about blockchain. *Harvard Business Review, 95*(1), 118–127.
MacDonald, T. J., Allen, D. W., & Potts, J. (2016). Blockchains and the boundaries of self-organized economies: Predictions for the future of banking. *Banking Beyond Banks and Money* (pp. 279–296). Cham: Springer.
Morkunas, V. J., Paschen, J., & Boon, E. (2019). How blockchain technologies impact your business model. *Business Horizons, 62*(3), 295–306.
Nakamoto, S. (2008). *Bitcoin: A peer-to-peer electronic cash* system. Available at: https://bitcoin.org/bitcoin.pdf.
Nowiński, W., & Kozma, M. (2017). How can blockchain technology disrupt the existing business models? *Entrepreneurial Business and Economics Review, 5*(3), 173–188.
Osterwalder, A., & Pigneur, Y. (2010). *Business model generation: a handbook for visionaries, game changers, and challengers*. John Wiley & Sons.
Peters, G. W., & Panayi, E. (2016). Understanding modern banking ledgers through blockchain technologies: Future of transaction processing and smart contracts on the internet of money. *Banking Beyond Banks and Money* (pp. 239–278). Cham: Springer.
Rajnak, V., & Puschmann, T. (2020). The impact of blockchain on business models in banking. *Information Systems and e-Business Management*, 1–53.
Stulz, R. M. (2019). FinTech, BigTech, and the future of banks. *Journal of Applied Corporate Finance, 31*(4), 86–97.
Swan, M. (2015). *Blockchain: Blueprint for a new economy*, O'Reilly Media, Inc., 1005 Gravenstein Highway North, Sebastopol, CA 95472.
Tapscott, A., & Tapscott, D. (2017). How blockchain is changing finance. *Harvard Business Review, 1*(9), 2–5.
Ulieru, M. (2016). Blockchain 2.0 and beyond: Adhocracies. In *Banking beyond banks and money* (pp. 297–303). Cham: Springer.
Walport, M. (2016). *Distributed ledger technology: Beyond blockchain*. UK Government Office for Science. Available at: https://assets.publishing.service.gov.uk/government/uploads/system/uploads/attachment_data/file/492972/gs-16-1-distributed-ledger-technology.pdf.
Yermack, D. (2017). Corporate governance and blockchains. *Review of Finance, 21*(1), 7–31.
Yermack, D. (2019, May 20). *Blockchain technology's potential in the financial system*. Prepared for the Federal Reserve Bank of Atlanta, 2019 Financial Market's Conference, Amelia Island, FL. Available at: https://www.frbatlanta.org/news/conferences-and-events/conferences/2019/0519-financial-markets-conference/-/media/1B59605EE1E946C6909F505A8341EB04.ashx.

Index

A

advantages, 4, 5, 10, 13, 15, 23, 24, 36, 39, 43, 45, 46, 48, 58, 63, 66
altcoins, 21
anonymity, 22, 23, 37, 72, 73
anti-money laundering (AML), 73, 76, 77, 80, 81, 83, 93
Anti-Money Laundering Directive (AMLD), 77
Asia, 3, 80
asymmetric cryptography, 12
Australia, 82, 83, 91, 92
Australian Securities and Investments Commission (ASIC), 83, 91, 92
automation, 16, 25, 26, 41

B

banking areas, 5, 34, 39, 40, 42, 49, 63, 84, 101, 103
banking business models, 4, 5, 53–55, 64–67, 101–103
banking efficiency, 38, 46, 49, 63
banking industry, 1–3, 5, 34, 35, 54, 55, 64, 67, 84, 93, 99–101
banking processes, 39, 45, 46, 49, 63, 84
banking services, 1, 4, 22, 35–37, 47, 49, 55, 57, 58, 63, 72, 101
banks, 2–5, 12, 20–22, 26, 34–49, 53–67, 71–73, 77, 84, 88, 92, 93, 99–103
bank's competitiveness, 36
banks' profitability, 4, 36–38, 49, 64, 66, 101, 103
Bitcoin, 3, 9, 13, 16–23, 34, 35, 38, 80, 82, 100
blockchain, 3–5, 9–13, 15–21, 23–26, 33–49, 54–67, 71–73, 80, 84–93, 100–103
Blockchain 1.0, 4, 18, 19, 34, 100
Blockchain 2.0, 4, 18, 19, 100
Blockchain 3.0, 18, 19
blockchain-based start-ups, 36, 100, 102
blockchain consortia, 64

P. Martino, *Blockchain and Banking*,
https://doi.org/10.1007/978-3-030-70970-9

Business Model Canvas (BMC), 5, 54–56, 64, 66, 101, 103
business model innovation, 2, 54, 55, 66
business models, 2, 4, 5, 33, 36, 37, 39, 45, 49, 54–56, 59–61, 63, 65–67, 76, 77, 100–103

C

capital markets, 40, 49, 58, 101
central banking systems, 20
centralised digital currency, 20
centralised systems, 15, 35, 100
challenges, 2, 4, 5, 16, 26, 34, 37, 42, 48, 58, 60–62, 64, 66, 67, 72, 73, 84–86, 92, 99, 101–103
channels, 5, 36, 56, 58, 66, 101
China, 81, 82, 90
clearing and settlement, 40, 82
Commodity Futures Trading Commission (CFTC), 74, 75
competition, 2, 4, 36, 55, 60, 61, 71, 99, 100
competitive edge, 4, 45, 47, 57, 60, 62, 63, 99, 101
compliance, 16, 26, 40, 43–45, 84, 85, 87, 90, 91, 93, 102
consensus mechanisms, 10, 13–15, 17, 21, 100
corporate lending, 40
cost structure, 56, 63
cross-border nature, 37, 72, 73
cryptocurrencies, 3–5, 9, 10, 14, 18, 20–24, 33–38, 48, 49, 58, 71–77, 80–83, 90, 92, 100
cryptography system, 11
currency, 14, 18, 19, 21–23, 43, 48, 76, 82, 83
customer relationship management (CRM), 59, 61, 102
customer relationships, 55, 56, 59
customer segments, 56–59

D

data analytics, 17, 38, 61, 102
data privacy, 88, 93
data protection, 45, 84–86, 88, 93
decentralisation, 15, 17, 19, 73, 85
decentralised, 10, 11, 17–19, 25, 35, 42, 44, 45, 62, 100
decentralised applications (Dapps), 19
decentralised control, 20
decentralised transaction processing, 11, 15
Delegated Proof of Stake (DPoS), 14
derivatives markets, 75
digital currencies, 2, 18, 20, 21, 48, 83
digital financial assets, 20
digital innovations, 2
digital platforms, 36
digital signature, 13
disadvantages, 4, 13, 15
disintermediation, 2, 15, 34, 35
disruptive technology, 3, 9, 10
distributed data storage, 10, 15, 100
distributed ledger, 10, 15, 18, 25, 44, 46, 60, 63, 65, 100, 102
distributed ledger technologies (DLTs), 2–5, 15, 25, 35, 38, 39, 44, 48, 49, 54–57, 59, 63–66, 72, 79, 80, 84, 87, 90–93, 101

E

efficiency, 2, 16, 18, 20, 34, 39–41, 44–46, 54, 59, 64, 65, 99, 101, 103
efficiency bottlenecks, 3, 39
efficiency improvements, 45, 71, 101
electronic payment system, 21, 35
emerging countries, 48
entrepreneurial finance, 23
Ethereum, 17, 19, 21, 25, 40, 41
Europe, 3, 43

European Banking Authority (EBA), 2, 55, 64, 65, 78, 79, 84, 86, 102
European Commission (EC), 77, 78, 80, 87
European Securities and Markets Authority (ESMA), 23, 78, 79, 84
European Supervisory Authorities (ESAs), 78
European Union (EU), 5, 45, 64, 72, 77–80, 84–87

F
Financial Crimes Enforcement Network (FinCEN), 74, 76, 77
financial inclusion, 22, 47, 48
financial institutions, 2–4, 18, 21, 26, 35, 39, 42–44, 46, 47, 77, 82, 90, 91, 102
financial markets, 2, 3, 9, 19, 71, 80, 100
financial services, 2, 3, 25, 26, 34, 36, 39, 45, 47, 54, 55, 58, 66, 73, 78, 83, 88, 90, 99, 100, 102
Financial Services Agency (FSA), 80, 81, 91
financial stability, 2, 80
Financial Stability Board (FSB), 2, 42, 43, 71, 92
financial system, 2, 46, 55, 62, 73
financial technology (fintech), 2, 3, 39, 62, 91, 99
fintech companies, 36
fintech start-ups, 4, 36, 55, 60, 62, 64, 92
fraud, 3, 16, 19, 20, 23, 24, 26, 37, 39, 43, 72–75, 82, 92
fundraising model, 23

G
General Data Protection Regulation (GDPR), 45, 84–86, 88
governments, 19, 20, 37, 66, 77, 80, 82, 83, 90–92, 102

H
hacking, 5, 23, 37, 72
hash functions, 11, 13
human resources, 60, 61, 92, 102
hybrid blockchains, 17, 18

I
illicit activities, 23, 24, 37, 72, 73, 92
immutability, 16, 26, 86
information asymmetry, 2
information technology (IT), 1, 46, 58, 60–62, 102
Initial Coin Offerings (ICOs), 23, 24, 74, 78, 81–83, 90
innovation, 2, 3, 9, 23, 34, 54, 55, 57, 60, 62–64, 90, 100–102
international money transfers, 39, 43, 63
interoperability, 46, 66, 87, 102

J
Japan, 41, 80, 81, 91

K
key activities, 56, 60, 61
key partnerships, 56, 61, 62
key resources, 46, 56, 59, 60, 62
know-your-customer (KYC), 40, 43–45, 47, 48, 58, 62, 73, 83, 84, 91

L
ledger, 10, 11, 13, 15, 17, 46, 57, 59, 60
lending, 2, 36, 38, 42, 49, 58, 101
loans, 19, 26, 40, 41, 59

M
manipulation, 37, 72, 73, 75, 92
medium of exchange, 20
money laundering, 20, 23, 37, 72, 73, 77, 92, 93

N
new market segments, 48, 54, 58, 63, 66, 101

O
operational cost, 39, 40, 43, 63
operational risks, 3, 39, 42
operations, 3, 4, 16, 19, 37–40, 42, 43, 53, 59, 63, 65, 84, 101
opportunities, 3–5, 24, 34, 47, 49, 55, 56, 58, 64, 72, 100, 101

P
partnership, 61, 62, 66, 76, 101
payments, 1, 4, 18–22, 26, 36, 41–43, 46, 58, 63, 71, 101
payment systems, 1, 19, 42, 49
peer-to-peer technology, 11
People's Bank of China (PBOC), 82, 90
permissioned blockchains, 17, 18, 38, 41, 49, 86
permissionless blockchains, 17, 21, 34, 86
pilots, 64, 80, 103
policymakers, 2, 20, 72
privacy, 2, 5, 17, 18, 22, 34, 39, 45, 84, 88, 91
private blockchains, 4, 16–18, 38, 41, 49, 72, 86, 93, 101
private key, 12, 13, 21, 22
product innovation, 63, 71, 101
Proof of Stake (PoS), 14
Proof of Work (PoW), 13, 14, 17, 21
proofs of concept (PoC), 64
pseudo-anonymity, 37, 72
public blockchains, 4, 16–18, 34, 38, 39, 72, 86, 100
public key, 12, 13, 21, 23

R
regulation, 5, 23, 24, 26, 27, 37, 38, 44, 72–74, 76–81, 83–85, 88, 90–93
regulators, 2, 23, 33, 37, 43, 44, 66, 72–74, 80, 82, 84, 85, 90–93, 102
regulatory compliance, 39, 63
regulatory framework, 66, 72, 75, 78, 79, 81, 84, 85, 87, 88, 91–93, 102
regulatory issues, 5, 16, 18, 26, 37, 39, 45, 49, 66, 72, 74, 84, 86, 91–93
research & development (R&D), 61, 90, 102
revenue streams, 47–49, 56, 58, 62, 63, 65, 101
risks, 2, 5, 10, 16, 17, 19, 24, 26, 34–38, 40, 49, 61, 64, 65, 71–73, 77, 80, 87, 88, 91, 92, 102

S
scalability, 16, 18, 22, 37–39, 66
Securities and Exchange Commission (SEC), 24, 36, 74, 75

securities trading, 39, 63, 80
securities transactions, 40, 75
security issues, 16, 22, 45, 84
smart contracts, 3, 4, 10, 16, 19, 20, 24–27, 33, 39, 41–43, 57, 62, 71, 84, 86, 87, 89–93
standardisation, 46, 66
supervisors, 2, 80
syndicated lending, 39, 63
syndicated loans, 41

T

tax evasion, 20, 23, 37, 72, 92
technological developments, 2, 5, 54, 66, 84, 90, 91, 102
technological innovations, 2, 53–55
tokens, 21, 23, 40, 80–83
trade finance, 26, 39, 41, 42, 49, 57, 58, 62, 63, 84, 93, 101
transaction lags, 3, 39
transparency, 10, 13, 16, 17, 19, 38, 39, 41, 73, 74

U

unbanked, 22, 47–49, 58, 63, 101
underbanked, 22, 47–49, 58, 63, 101
United States (US), 3, 5, 26, 37, 72–75, 77, 87–89
universities, 62, 66, 102

V

value proposition, 54, 56–61, 64–66, 101, 103
virtual currency, 18, 23, 73, 75–77, 81, 82

The manufacturer's authorised representative in the EU is Springer Nature Customer Service Centre GmbH, Europaplatz 3, 69115 Heidelberg, Germany. If you have any concerns regarding our products, please contact ProductSafety@springernature.com

Printed and bound by CPI Group (UK) Ltd, Croydon, CR0 4YY
24/09/2026
02222057-0003